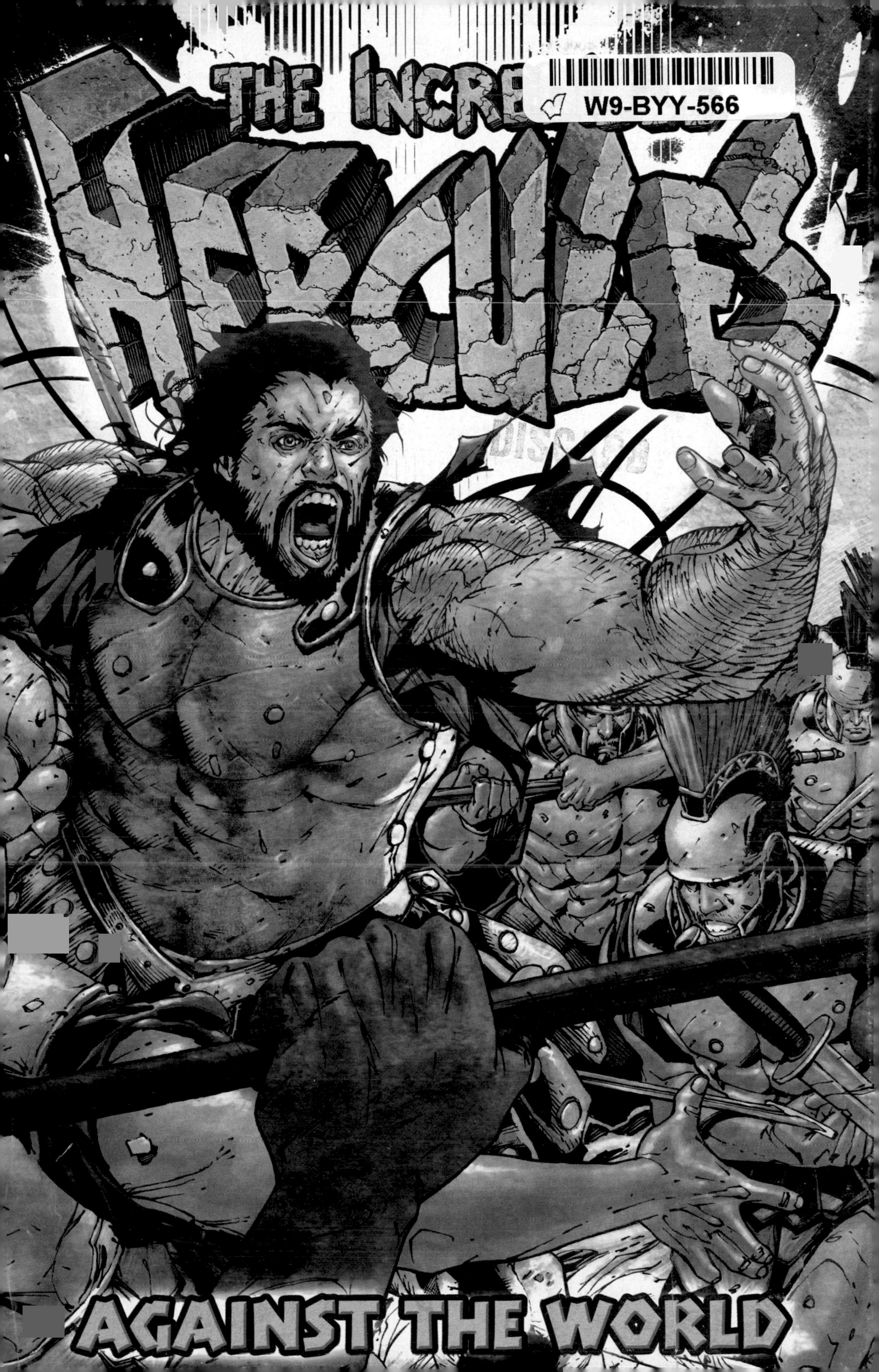
AGAINST THE WORLD

THE INCREDIBLE HERCULES

Writers: **GREG PAK** & **FRED VAN LENTE**

INCREDIBLE HULK #112 & INCREDIBLE HERCULES #113-115
Penciler: **KHOI PHAM**
Inkers: **KHOI PHAM** (Issue #112) • **PAUL NEARY** (Issue # 113-114)
PAUL NEARY with **DANNY MIKI** (Issue #115)
Colorists: **STEPHANE PERU** (Issue #112-114) & **DENNIS CALERO** (Issue #115)
Letterers: **CHRIS ELIOPOULOS** & **VC'S JOE CARAMAGNA**
Cover Artists: **ARTHUR ADAMS** & **LAURA MARTIN** (Issue #112)
ARTHUR ADAMS & **GURU EFX** (Issue #113-115)

HULK VS. HERCULES: WHEN TITANS COLLIDE
Artists: **KHOI PHAM, PAUL NEARY** & **DENNIS CALERO** (Pages 1-2, 31)
ERIC NGUYEN (Pages 3-7) • **REILLY BROWN, CARLOS CUEVAS,**
TERRY PALLOT & **CHRIS SOTOMAYOR** (Pages 8, 11-30)
BOB LAYTON & **GURU EFX** (Pages 9-10)
Letterer: **VC'S JOE CARAMAGNA**
Cover Artist: **MARKO DJURDJEVIC**

Assistant Editor: **NATHAN COSBY**
Editor: **MARK PANICCIA**

Collection Editor: **CORY LEVINE**
Editorial Assistant: **JODY LEHEUP** • Assistant Editor: **JOHN DENNING**
Editors, Special Projects: **JENNIFER GRÜNWALD** & **MARK D. BEAZLEY**
Senior Editor, Special Projects: **JEFF YOUNGQUIST**
Senior Vice President of Sales: **DAVID GABRIEL**
Book Design: **RODOLFO MURAGUCHI**

Editor in Chief: **JOE QUESADA** • Publisher: **DAN BUCKLEY**

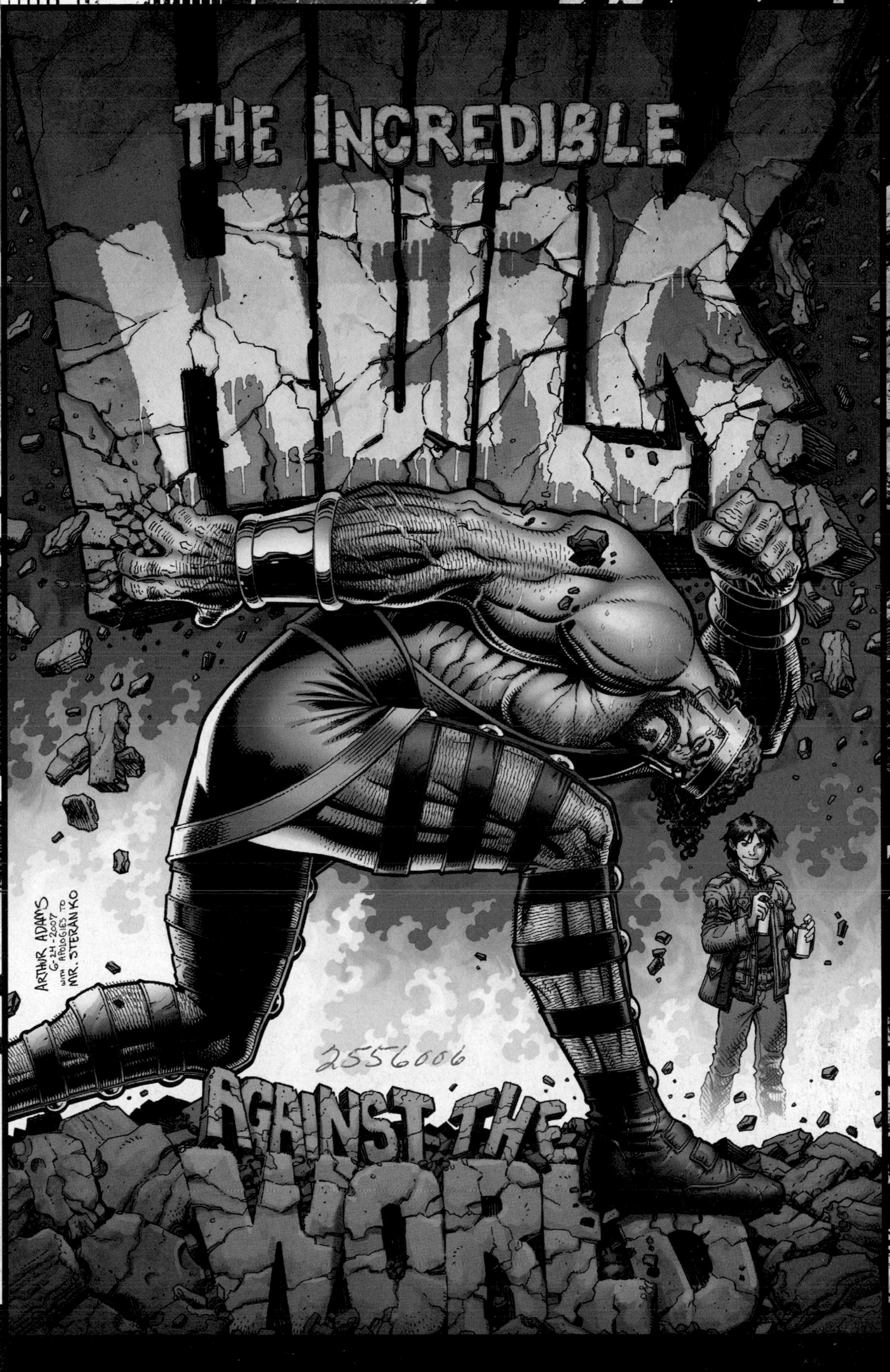
THE INCREDIBLE
HULK
ARTHUR ADAMS 6-24-2007 WITH APOLOGIES TO MR. STERANKO
2556006
AGAINST THE
WORLD

INCREDIBLE HULK #112

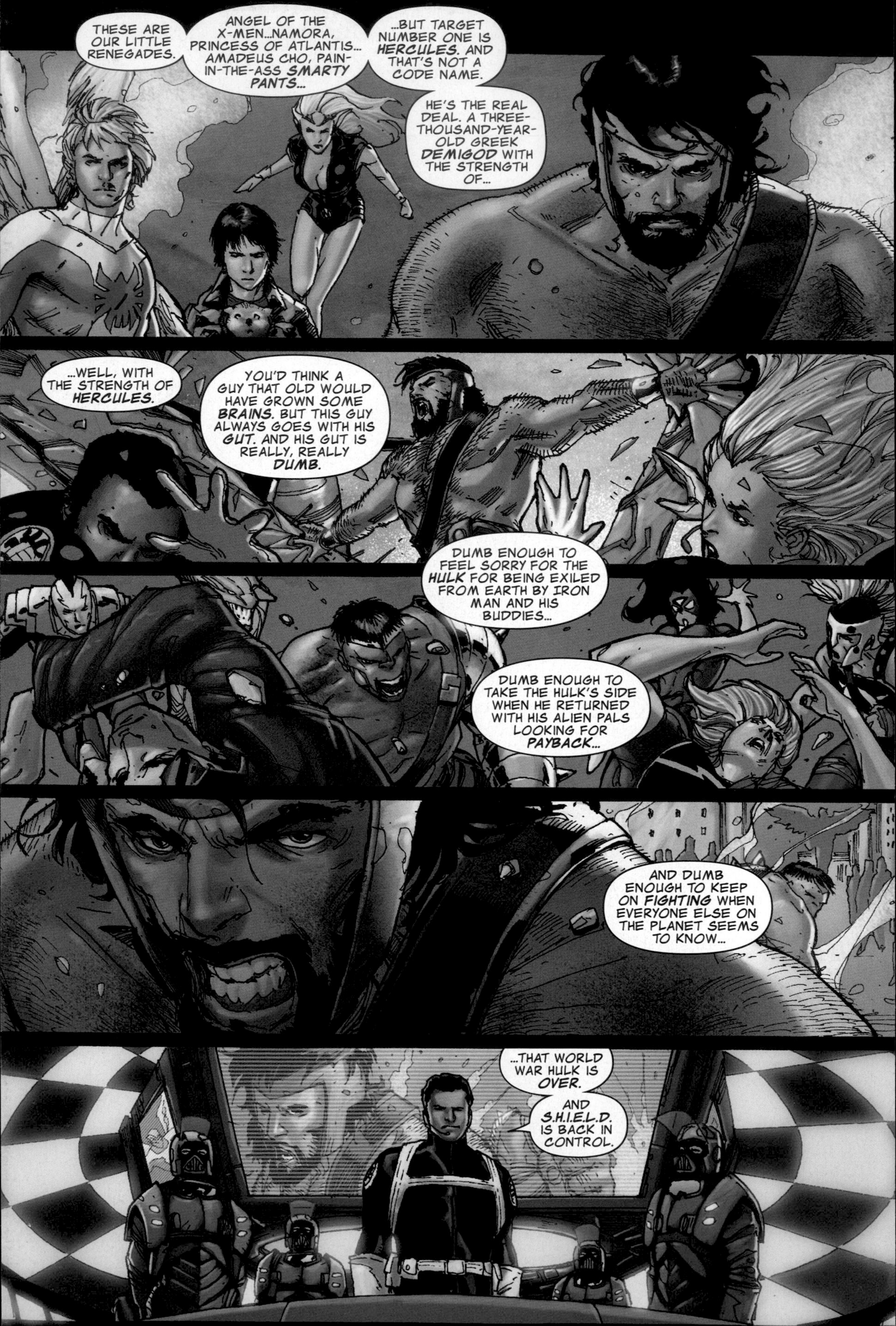
THESE ARE OUR LITTLE RENEGADES.
ANGEL OF THE X-MEN...NAMORA, PRINCESS OF ATLANTIS... AMADEUS CHO, PAIN-IN-THE-ASS SMARTY PANTS...
...BUT TARGET NUMBER ONE IS HERCULES. AND THAT'S NOT A CODE NAME.
HE'S THE REAL DEAL. A THREE-THOUSAND-YEAR-OLD GREEK DEMIGOD WITH THE STRENGTH OF...
...WELL, WITH THE STRENGTH OF HERCULES.
YOU'D THINK A GUY THAT OLD WOULD HAVE GROWN SOME BRAINS. BUT THIS GUY ALWAYS GOES WITH HIS GUT. AND HIS GUT IS REALLY, REALLY DUMB.
DUMB ENOUGH TO FEEL SORRY FOR THE HULK FOR BEING EXILED FROM EARTH BY IRON MAN AND HIS BUDDIES...
DUMB ENOUGH TO TAKE THE HULK'S SIDE WHEN HE RETURNED WITH HIS ALIEN PALS LOOKING FOR PAYBACK...
AND DUMB ENOUGH TO KEEP ON FIGHTING WHEN EVERYONE ELSE ON THE PLANET SEEMS TO KNOW...
...THAT WORLD WAR HULK IS OVER.
AND S.H.I.E.L.D. IS BACK IN CONTROL.

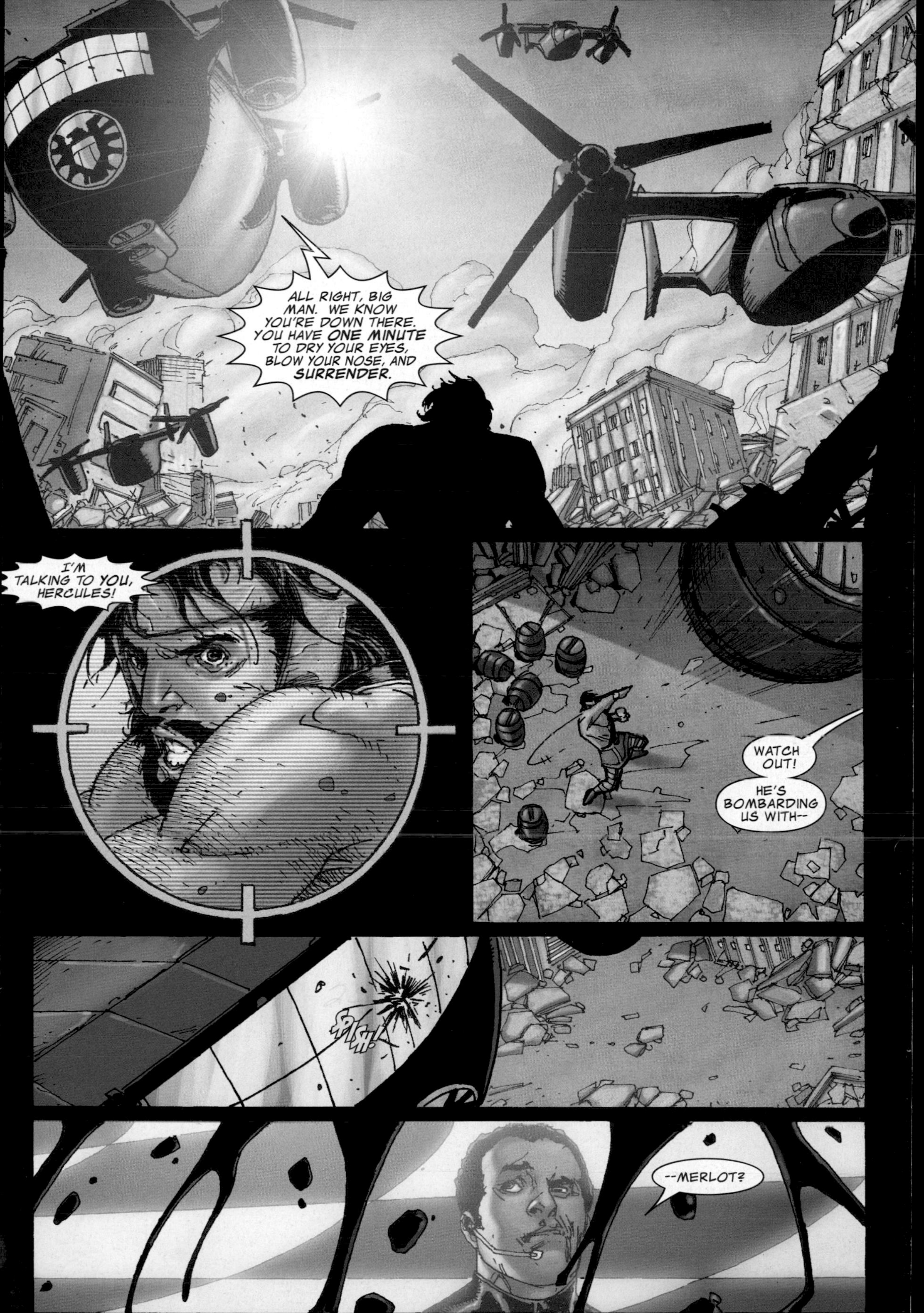
ALL RIGHT, BIG MAN. WE KNOW YOU'RE DOWN THERE. YOU HAVE ONE MINUTE TO DRY YOUR EYES, BLOW YOUR NOSE, AND SURRENDER.
I'M TALKING TO YOU, HERCULES!
WATCH OUT! HE'S BOMBARDING US WITH--
SPISH!
--MERLOT?

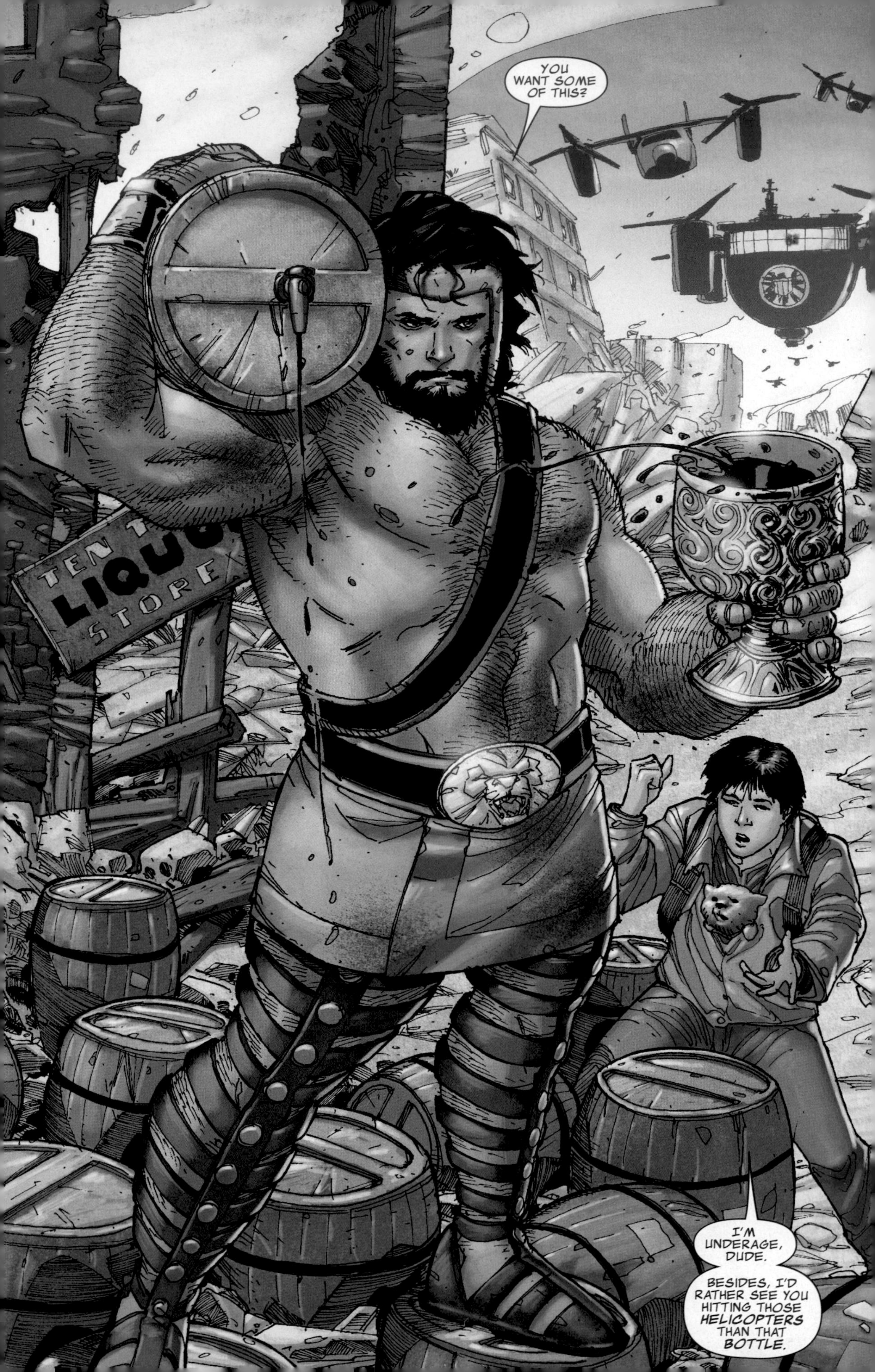
YOU WANT SOME OF THIS?
TEN
LIQU
STORE
I'M UNDERAGE, DUDE.
BESIDES, I'D RATHER SEE YOU HITTING THOSE HELICOPTERS THAN THAT BOTTLE.

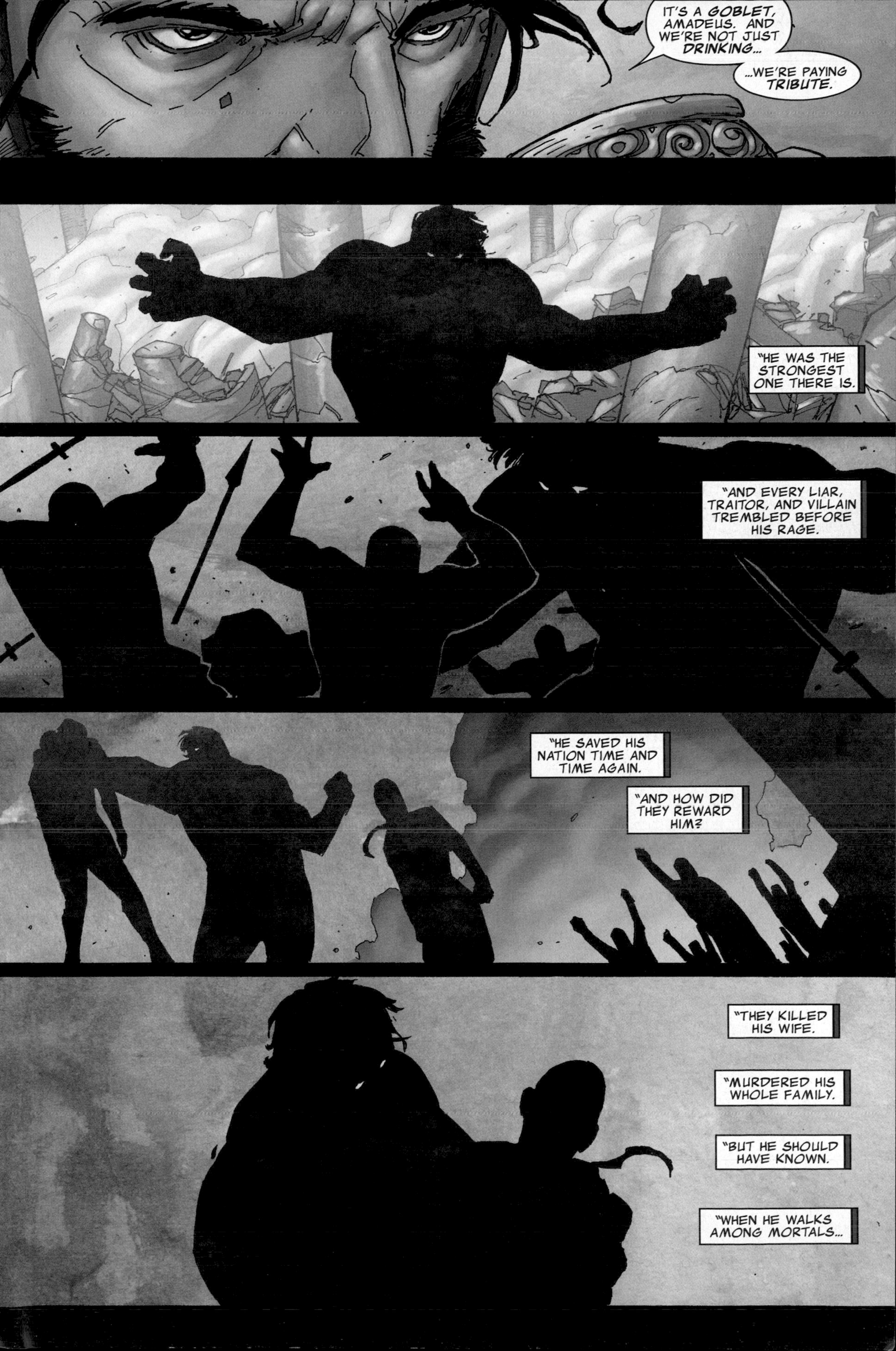
IT'S A GOBLET, AMADEUS. AND WE'RE NOT JUST DRINKING...
...WE'RE PAYING TRIBUTE.
"HE WAS THE STRONGEST ONE THERE IS.
"AND EVERY LIAR, TRAITOR, AND VILLAIN TREMBLED BEFORE HIS RAGE.
"HE SAVED HIS NATION TIME AND TIME AGAIN.
"AND HOW DID THEY REWARD HIM?
"THEY KILLED HIS WIFE.
"MURDERED HIS WHOLE FAMILY.
"BUT HE SHOULD HAVE KNOWN.
"WHEN HE WALKS AMONG MORTALS...

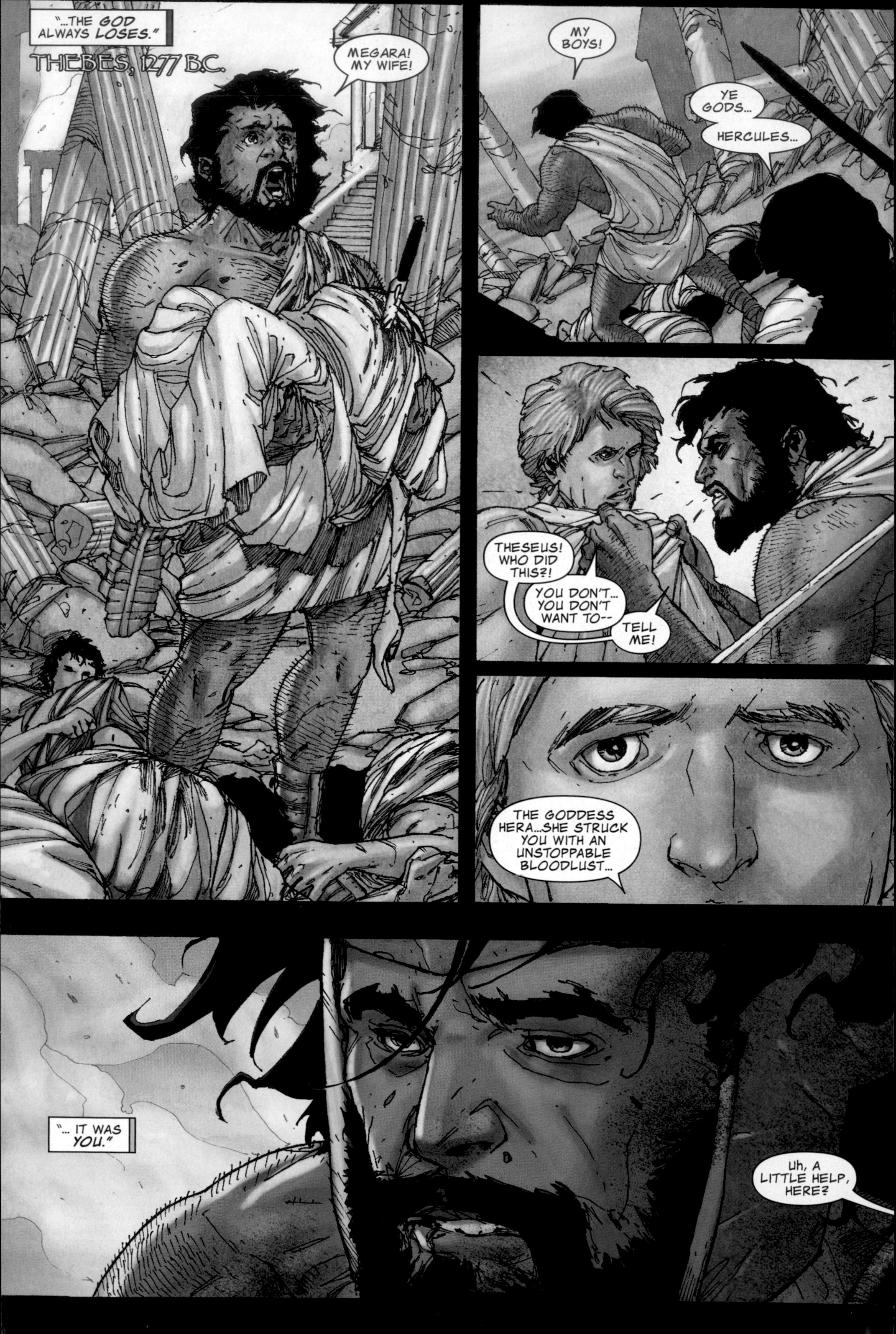
"...THE GOD ALWAYS LOSES."
THEBES, 1277 B.C.
MEGARA! MY WIFE!
MY BOYS!
YE GODS...
HERCULES...
THESEUS! WHO DID THIS?!
YOU DON'T... YOU DON'T WANT TO--
TELL ME!
THE GODDESS HERA...SHE STRUCK YOU WITH AN UNSTOPPABLE BLOODLUST...
"... IT WAS YOU."
UH, A LITTLE HELP, HERE?

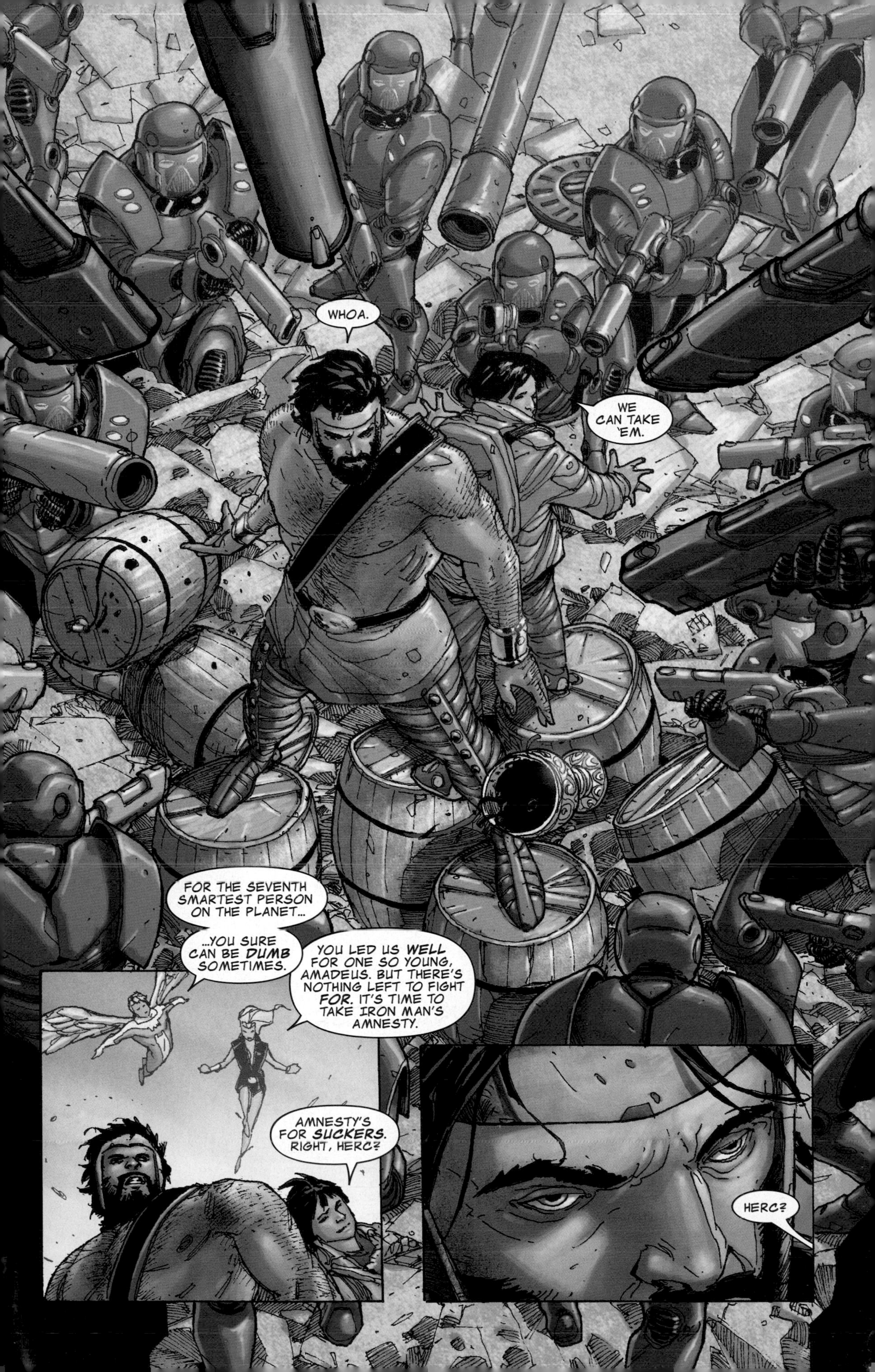
WHOA.
WE CAN TAKE 'EM.
FOR THE SEVENTH SMARTEST PERSON ON THE PLANET...
...YOU SURE CAN BE DUMB SOMETIMES.
YOU LED US WELL FOR ONE SO YOUNG, AMADEUS. BUT THERE'S NOTHING LEFT TO FIGHT FOR. IT'S TIME TO TAKE IRON MAN'S AMNESTY.
AMNESTY'S FOR SUCKERS. RIGHT, HERC?
HERC?

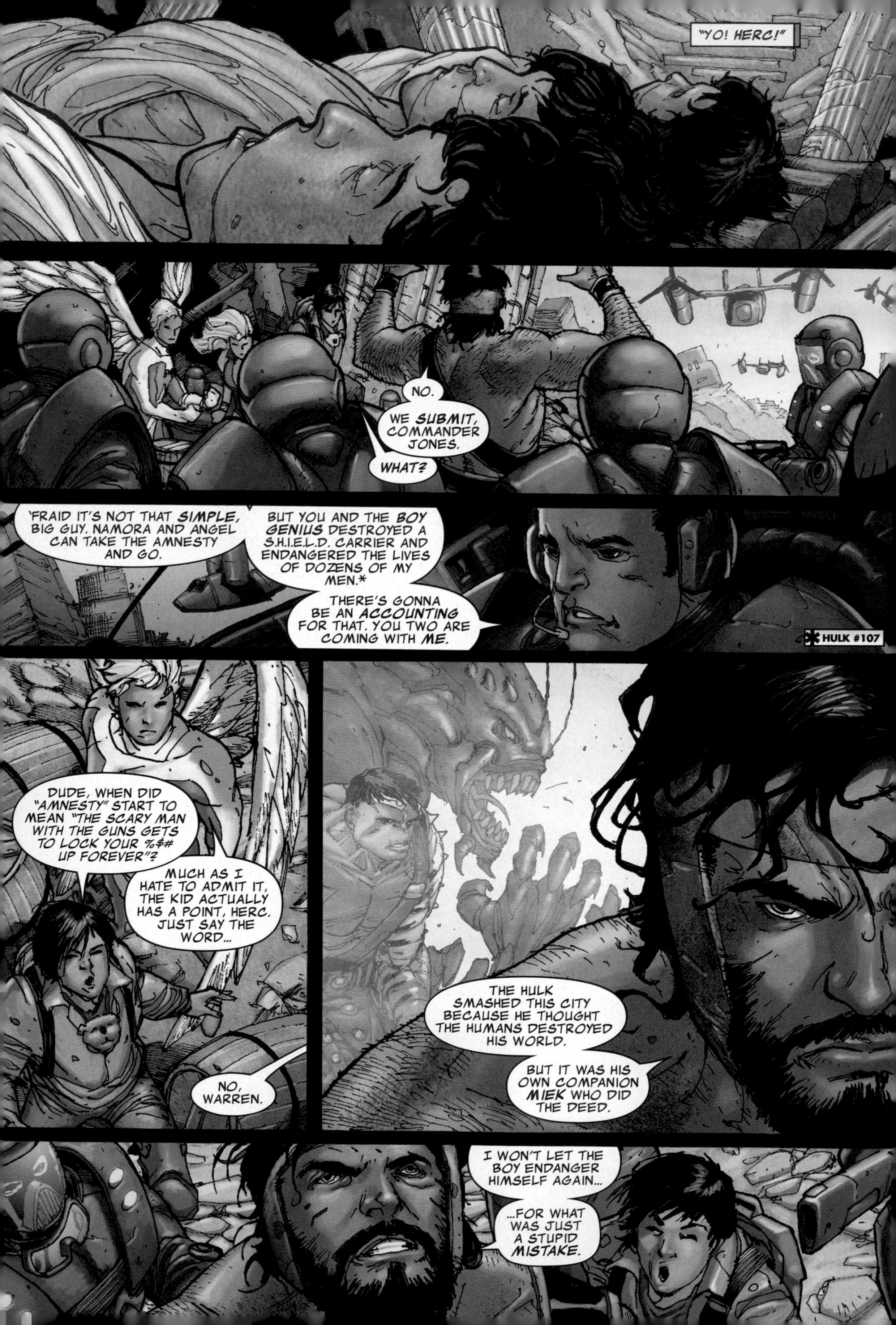
"YO! HERC!"
NO.
WE SUBMIT, COMMANDER JONES.
WHAT?
'FRAID IT'S NOT THAT SIMPLE, BIG GUY. NAMORA AND ANGEL CAN TAKE THE AMNESTY AND GO.
BUT YOU AND THE BOY GENIUS DESTROYED A S.H.I.E.L.D. CARRIER AND ENDANGERED THE LIVES OF DOZENS OF MY MEN.*
THERE'S GONNA BE AN ACCOUNTING FOR THAT. YOU TWO ARE COMING WITH ME.
* HULK #107
DUDE, WHEN DID "AMNESTY" START TO MEAN "THE SCARY MAN WITH THE GUNS GETS TO LOCK YOUR %$# UP FOREVER"?
MUCH AS I HATE TO ADMIT IT, THE KID ACTUALLY HAS A POINT, HERC. JUST SAY THE WORD...
NO, WARREN.
THE HULK SMASHED THIS CITY BECAUSE HE THOUGHT THE HUMANS DESTROYED HIS WORLD.
BUT IT WAS HIS OWN COMPANION MIEK WHO DID THE DEED.
I WON'T LET THE BOY ENDANGER HIMSELF AGAIN...
...FOR WHAT WAS JUST A STUPID MISTAKE.

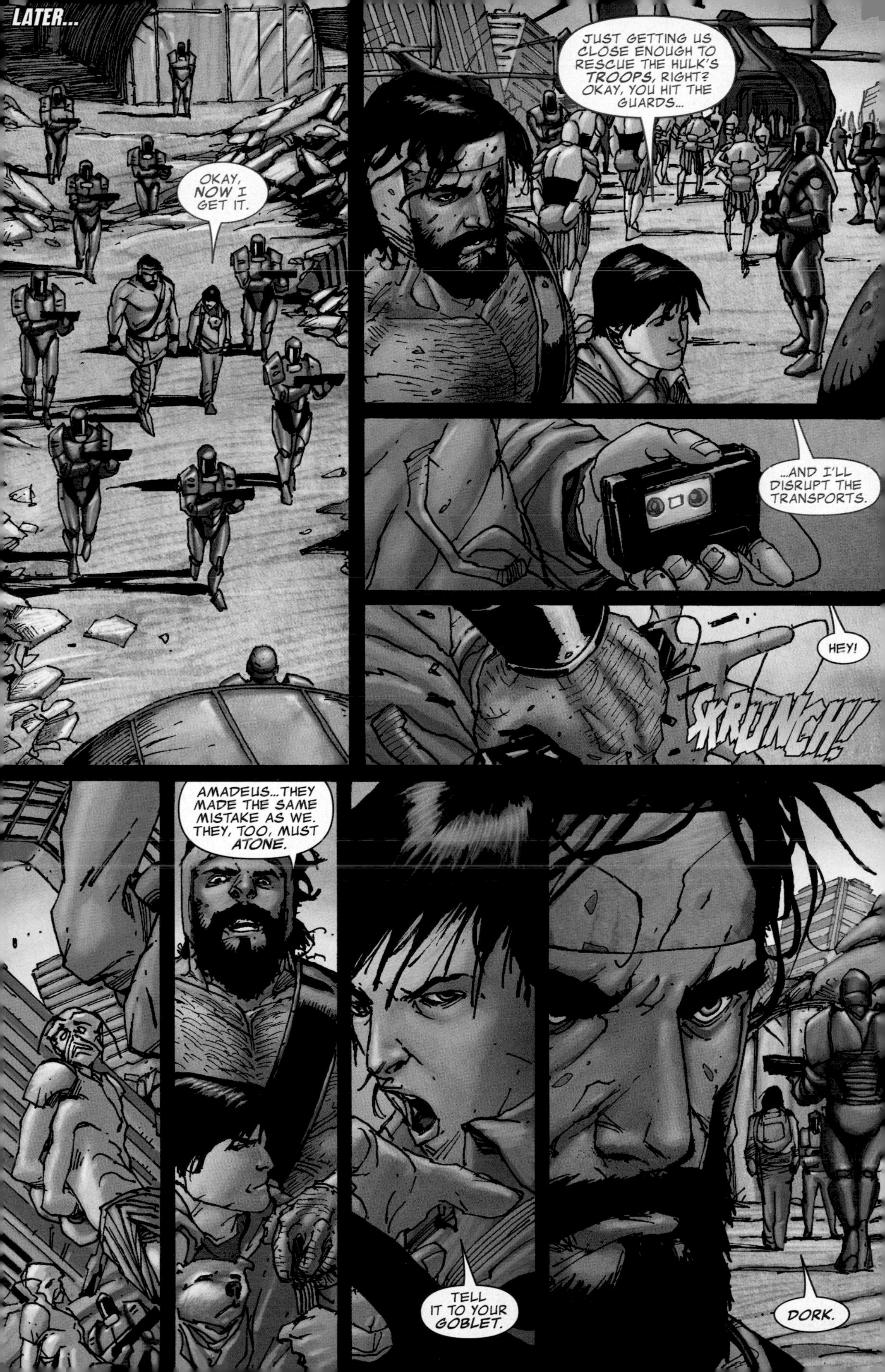
LATER...
OKAY, NOW I GET IT.
JUST GETTING US CLOSE ENOUGH TO RESCUE THE HULK'S TROOPS, RIGHT? OKAY, YOU HIT THE GUARDS...
...AND I'LL DISRUPT THE TRANSPORTS.
HEY!
SKRUNCH!
AMADEUS...THEY MADE THE SAME MISTAKE AS WE. THEY, TOO, MUST ATONE.
TELL IT TO YOUR GOBLET.
DORK.

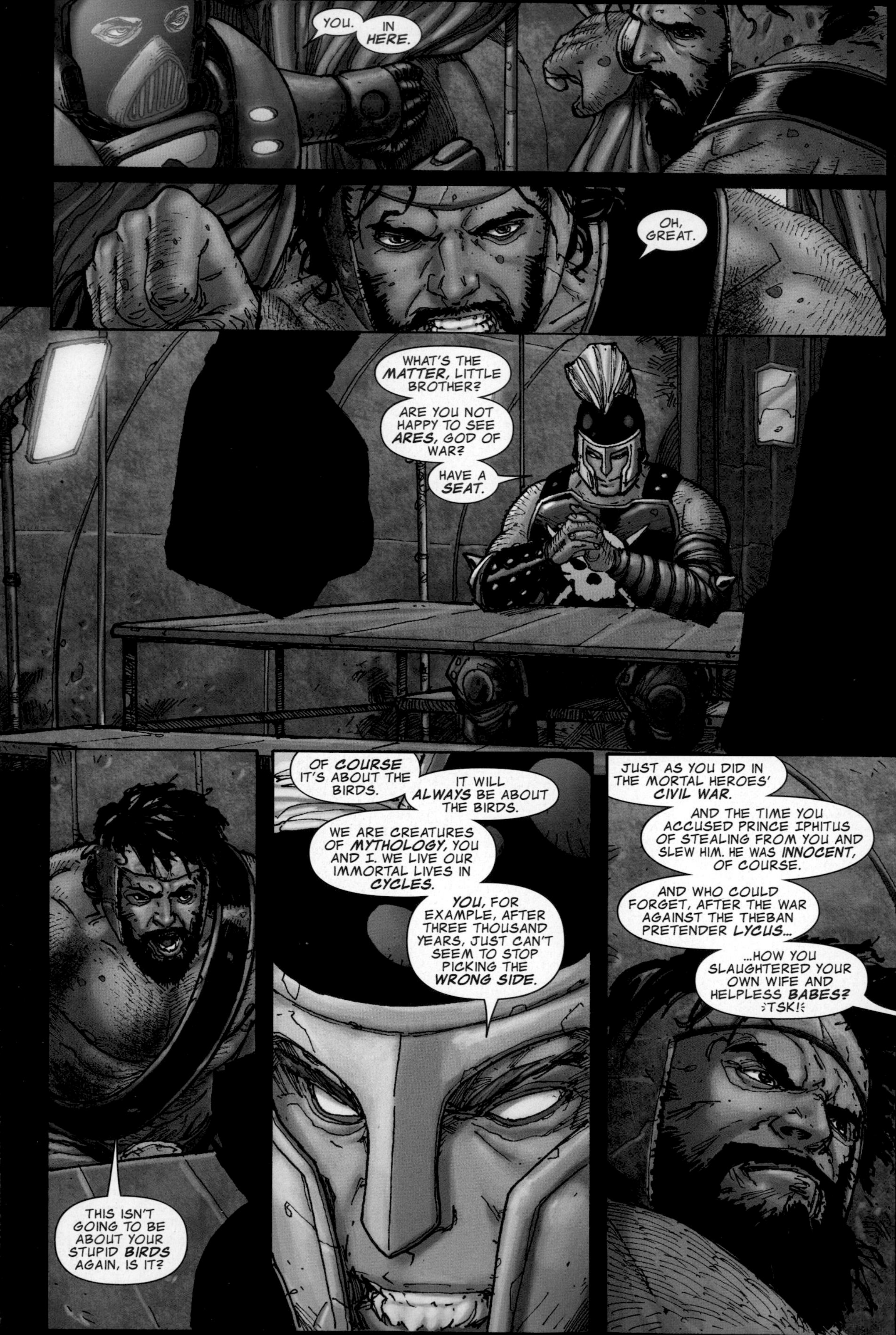
YOU.
IN HERE.
OH, GREAT.
WHAT'S THE MATTER, LITTLE BROTHER?
ARE YOU NOT HAPPY TO SEE ARES, GOD OF WAR?
HAVE A SEAT.
THIS ISN'T GOING TO BE ABOUT YOUR STUPID BIRDS AGAIN, IS IT?
OF COURSE IT'S ABOUT THE BIRDS.
IT WILL ALWAYS BE ABOUT THE BIRDS.
WE ARE CREATURES OF MYTHOLOGY, YOU AND I. WE LIVE OUR IMMORTAL LIVES IN CYCLES.
YOU, FOR EXAMPLE, AFTER THREE THOUSAND YEARS, JUST CAN'T SEEM TO STOP PICKING THE WRONG SIDE.
JUST AS YOU DID IN THE MORTAL HEROES' CIVIL WAR.
AND THE TIME YOU ACCUSED PRINCE IPHITUS OF STEALING FROM YOU AND SLEW HIM. HE WAS INNOCENT, OF COURSE.
AND WHO COULD FORGET, AFTER THE WAR AGAINST THE THEBAN PRETENDER LYCUS...
...HOW YOU SLAUGHTERED YOUR OWN WIFE AND HELPLESS BABES? TSK!

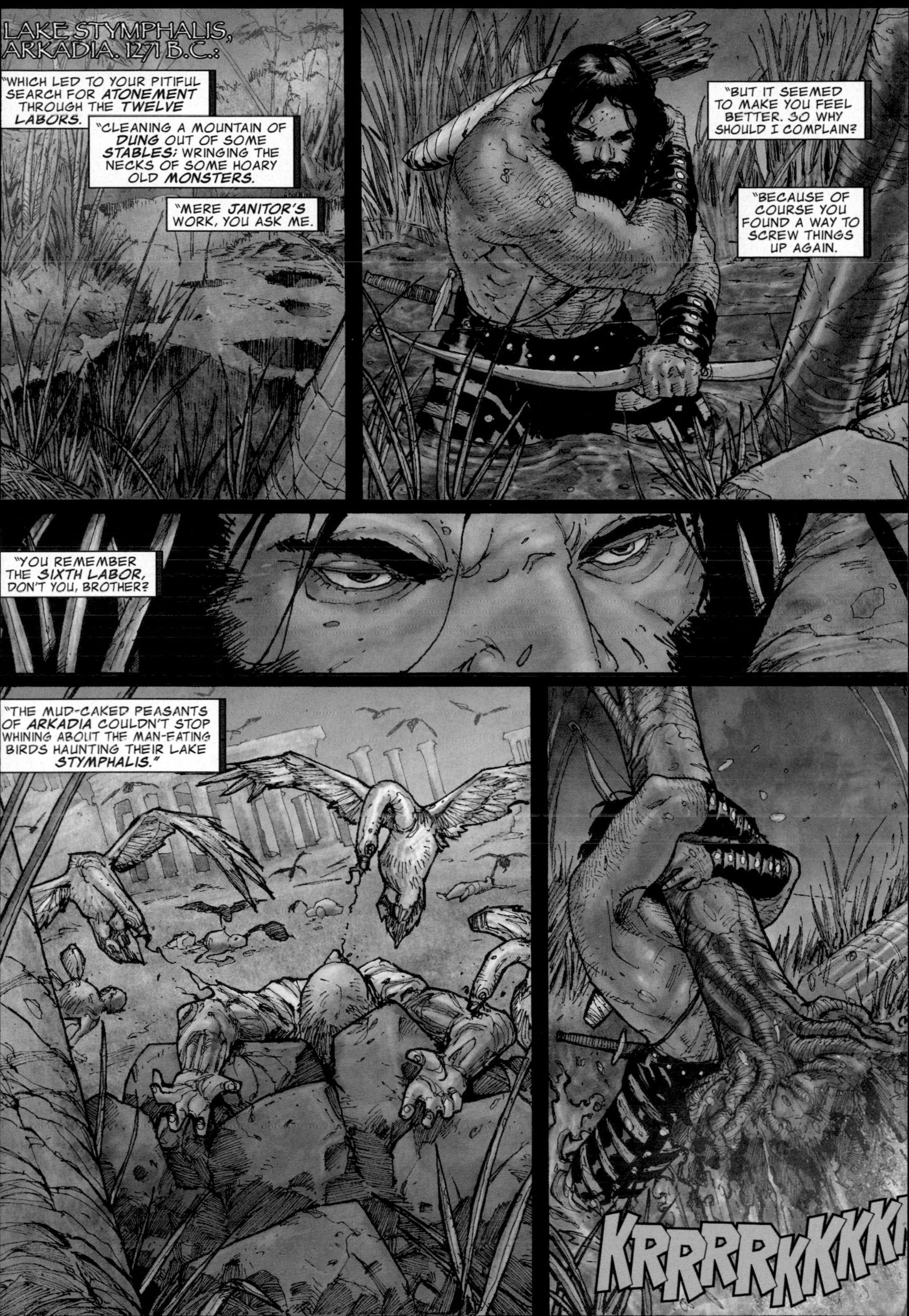
LAKE STYMPHALIS, ARKADIA. 1271 B.C.:
"WHICH LED TO YOUR PITIFUL SEARCH FOR ATONEMENT THROUGH THE TWELVE LABORS.
"CLEANING A MOUNTAIN OF DUNG OUT OF SOME STABLES; WRINGING THE NECKS OF SOME HOARY OLD MONSTERS.
"MERE JANITOR'S WORK, YOU ASK ME.
"BUT IT SEEMED TO MAKE YOU FEEL BETTER. SO WHY SHOULD I COMPLAIN?
"BECAUSE OF COURSE YOU FOUND A WAY TO SCREW THINGS UP AGAIN.
"YOU REMEMBER THE SIXTH LABOR, DON'T YOU, BROTHER?
"THE MUD-CAKED PEASANTS OF ARKADIA COULDN'T STOP WHINING ABOUT THE MAN-EATING BIRDS HAUNTING THEIR LAKE STYMPHALIS."
KRRRRKKKK

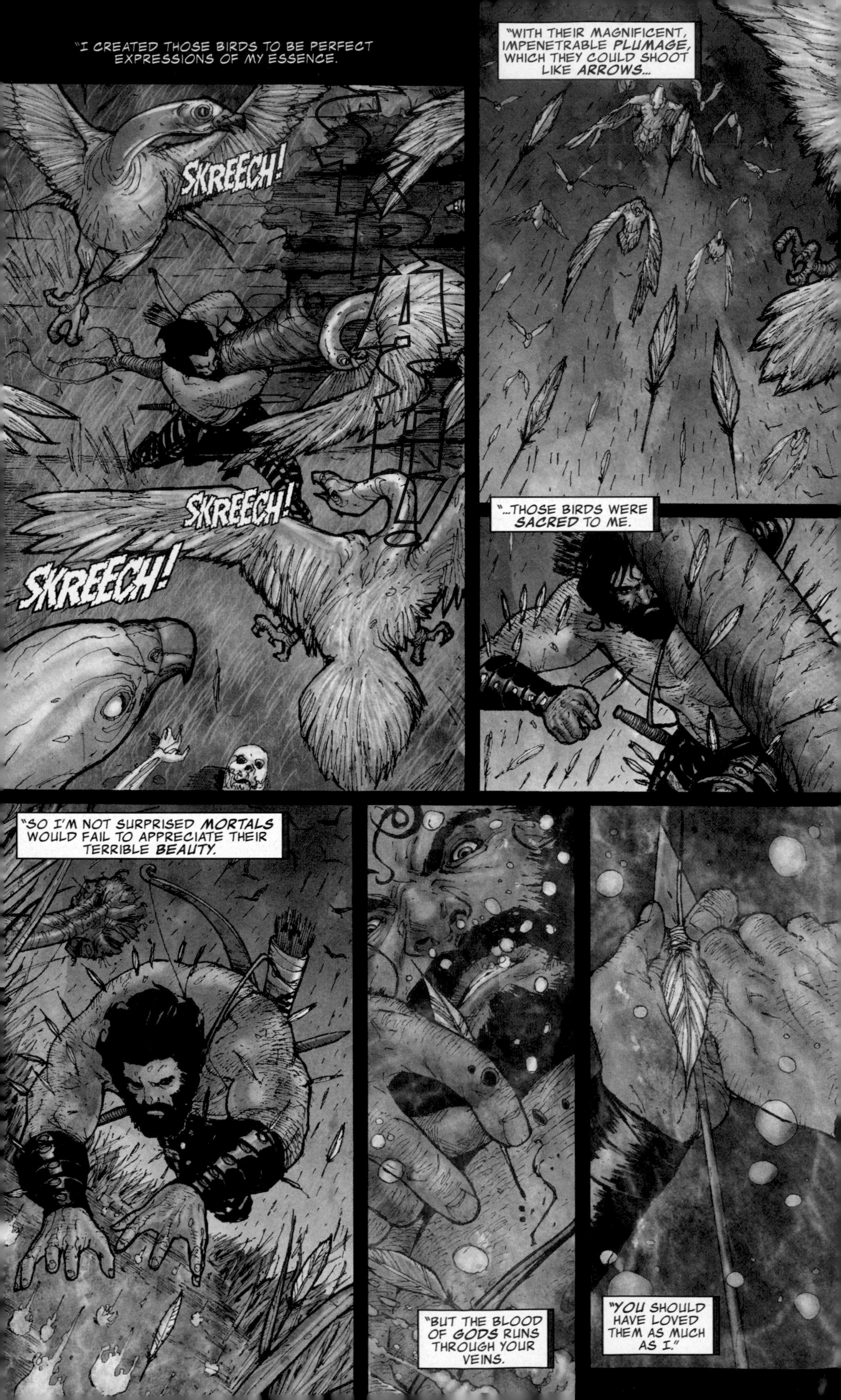
"I CREATED THOSE BIRDS TO BE PERFECT EXPRESSIONS OF MY ESSENCE.
SKREECH!
SKREECH!
SKREECH!
"WITH THEIR MAGNIFICENT, IMPENETRABLE PLUMAGE, WHICH THEY COULD SHOOT LIKE ARROWS...
"...THOSE BIRDS WERE SACRED TO ME.
"SO I'M NOT SURPRISED MORTALS WOULD FAIL TO APPRECIATE THEIR TERRIBLE BEAUTY.
"BUT THE BLOOD OF GODS RUNS THROUGH YOUR VEINS.
"YOU SHOULD HAVE LOVED THEM AS MUCH AS I."

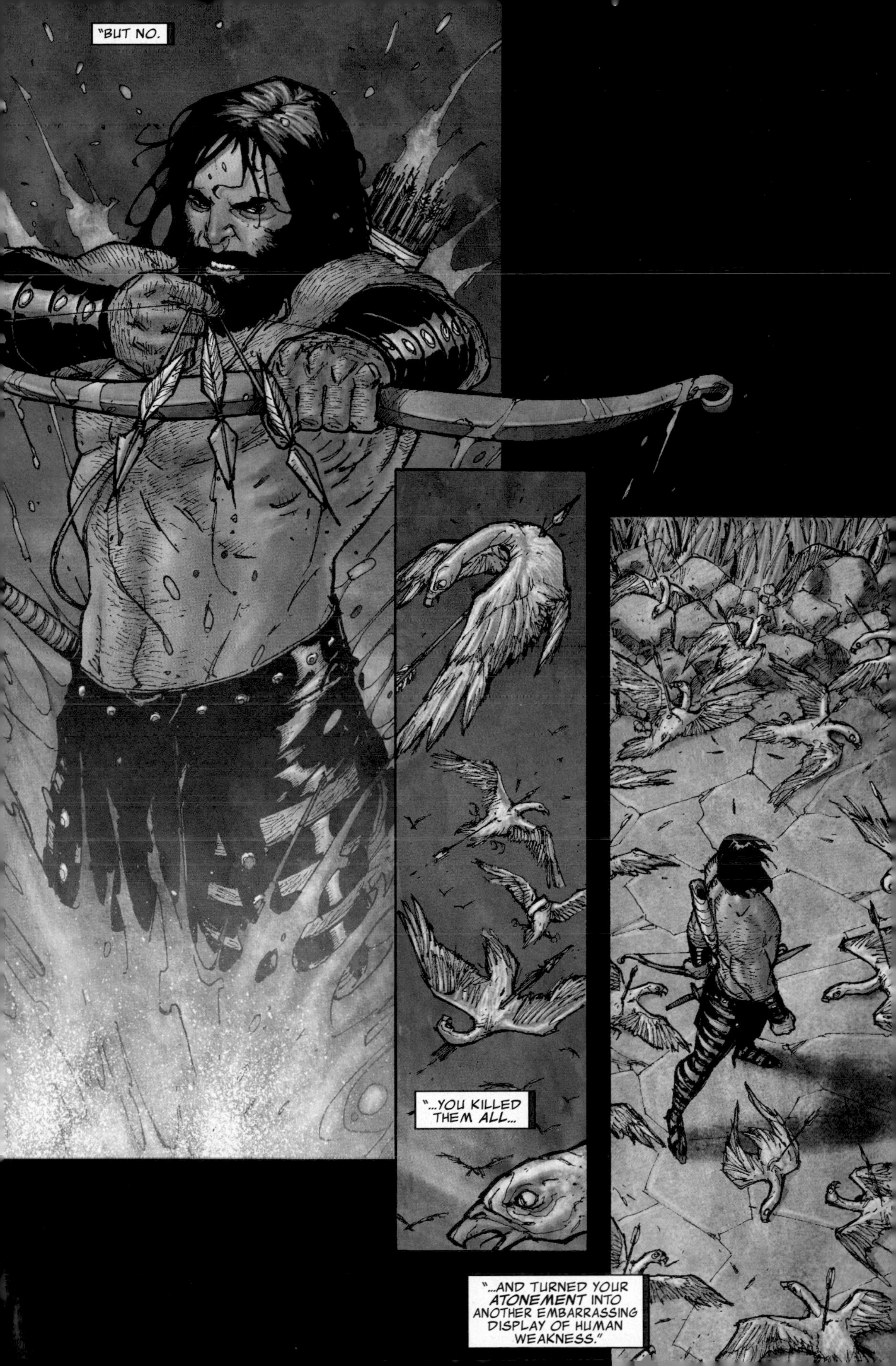
"BUT NO.
"...YOU KILLED THEM ALL...
"...AND TURNED YOUR ATONEMENT INTO ANOTHER EMBARRASSING DISPLAY OF HUMAN WEAKNESS."

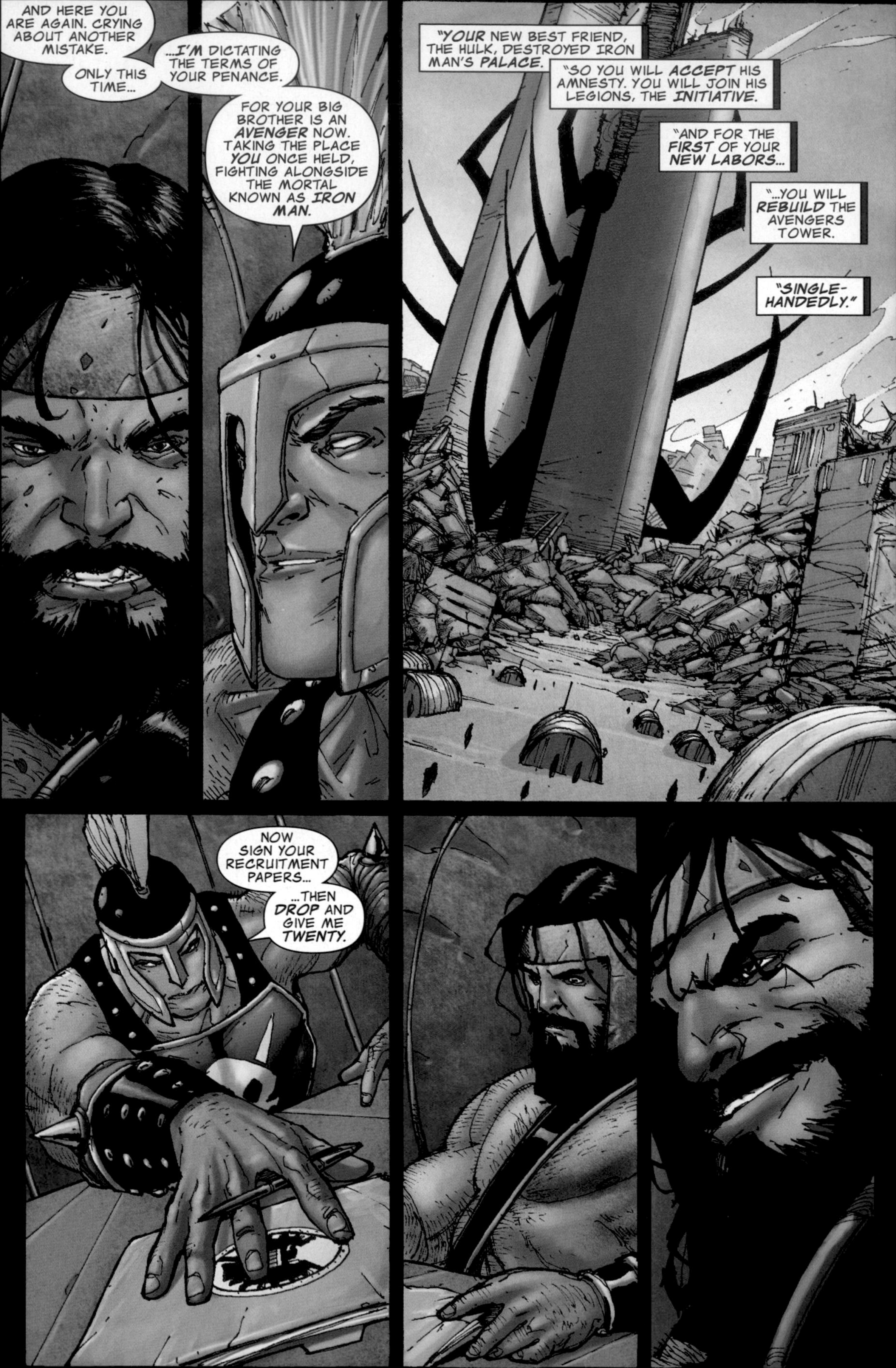

AND HERE YOU ARE AGAIN. CRYING ABOUT ANOTHER MISTAKE.
ONLY THIS TIME...
...I'M DICTATING THE TERMS OF YOUR PENANCE.
FOR YOUR BIG BROTHER IS AN AVENGER NOW. TAKING THE PLACE YOU ONCE HELD, FIGHTING ALONGSIDE THE MORTAL KNOWN AS IRON MAN.
"YOUR NEW BEST FRIEND, THE HULK, DESTROYED IRON MAN'S PALACE.
"SO YOU WILL ACCEPT HIS AMNESTY. YOU WILL JOIN HIS LEGIONS, THE INITIATIVE.
"AND FOR THE FIRST OF YOUR NEW LABORS...
"...YOU WILL REBUILD THE AVENGERS TOWER.
"SINGLE-HANDEDLY."
NOW SIGN YOUR RECRUITMENT PAPERS...
...THEN DROP AND GIVE ME TWENTY.

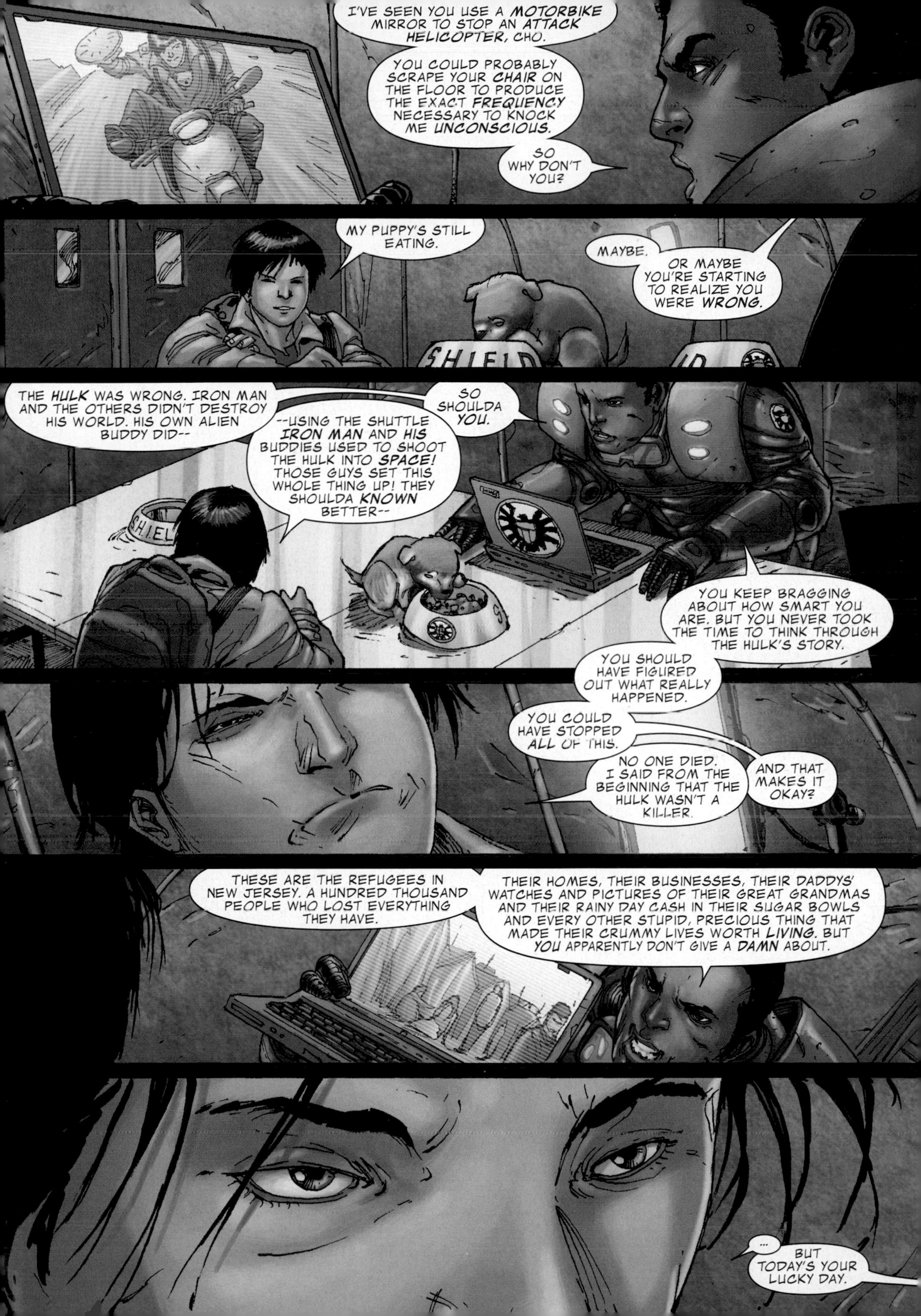
I'VE SEEN YOU USE A MOTORBIKE MIRROR TO STOP AN ATTACK HELICOPTER, CHO.
YOU COULD PROBABLY SCRAPE YOUR CHAIR ON THE FLOOR TO PRODUCE THE EXACT FREQUENCY NECESSARY TO KNOCK ME UNCONSCIOUS.
SO WHY DON'T YOU?
MY PUPPY'S STILL EATING.
MAYBE.
OR MAYBE YOU'RE STARTING TO REALIZE YOU WERE WRONG.
THE HULK WAS WRONG. IRON MAN AND THE OTHERS DIDN'T DESTROY HIS WORLD. HIS OWN ALIEN BUDDY DID--
SO SHOULDA YOU.
--USING THE SHUTTLE IRON MAN AND HIS BUDDIES USED TO SHOOT THE HULK INTO SPACE! THOSE GUYS SET THIS WHOLE THING UP! THEY SHOULDA KNOWN BETTER--
YOU KEEP BRAGGING ABOUT HOW SMART YOU ARE. BUT YOU NEVER TOOK THE TIME TO THINK THROUGH THE HULK'S STORY.
YOU SHOULD HAVE FIGURED OUT WHAT REALLY HAPPENED.
YOU COULD HAVE STOPPED ALL OF THIS.
NO ONE DIED. I SAID FROM THE BEGINNING THAT THE HULK WASN'T A KILLER.
AND THAT MAKES IT OKAY?
THESE ARE THE REFUGEES IN NEW JERSEY. A HUNDRED THOUSAND PEOPLE WHO LOST EVERYTHING THEY HAVE.
THEIR HOMES, THEIR BUSINESSES, THEIR DADDYS' WATCHES AND PICTURES OF THEIR GREAT GRANDMAS AND THEIR RAINY DAY CASH IN THEIR SUGAR BOWLS AND EVERY OTHER STUPID, PRECIOUS THING THAT MADE THEIR CRUMMY LIVES WORTH LIVING. BUT YOU APPARENTLY DON'T GIVE A DAMN ABOUT.
...
BUT TODAY'S YOUR LUCKY DAY.

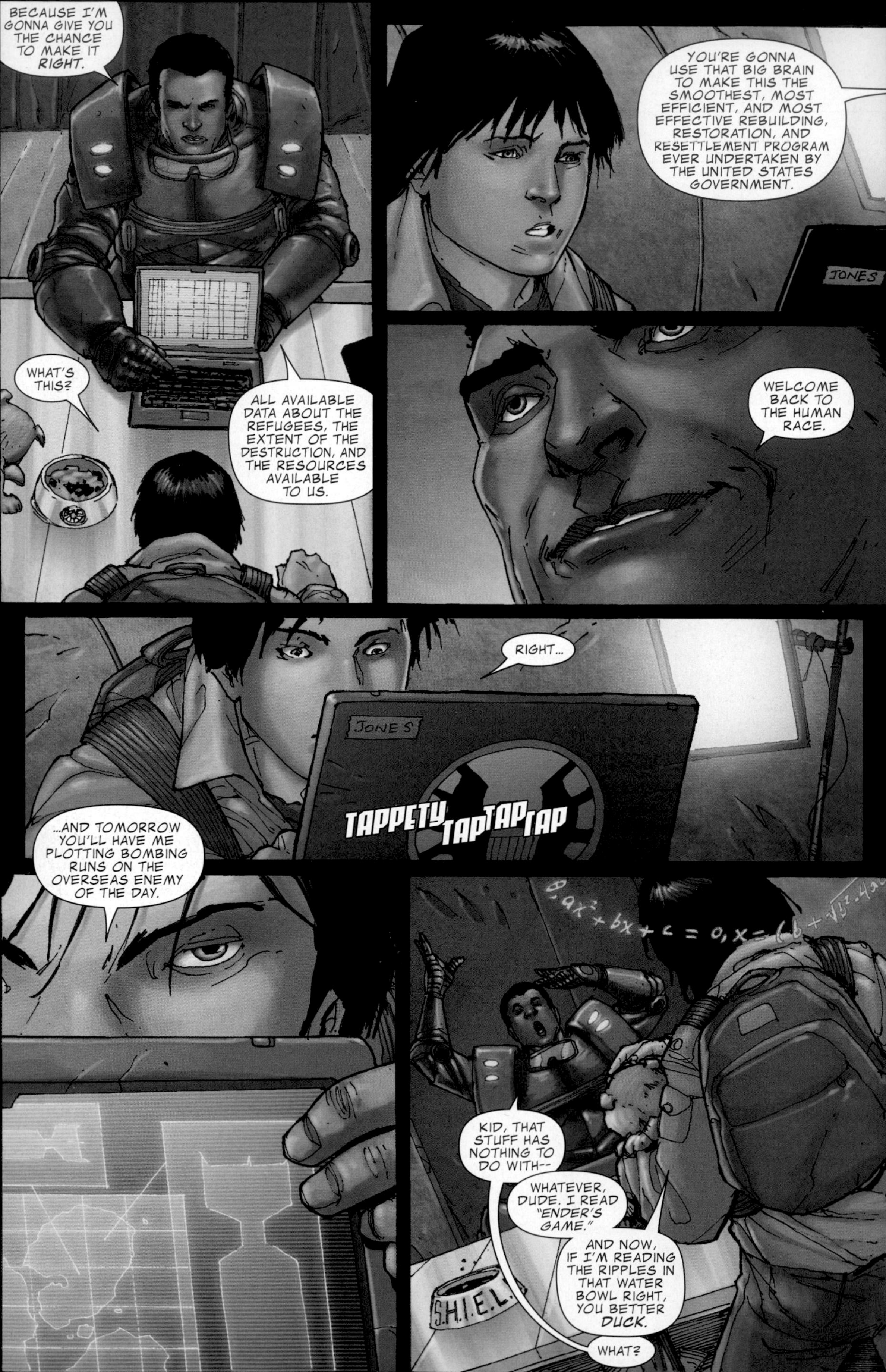
BECAUSE I'M GONNA GIVE YOU THE CHANCE TO MAKE IT RIGHT.
YOU'RE GONNA USE THAT BIG BRAIN TO MAKE THIS THE SMOOTHEST, MOST EFFICIENT, AND MOST EFFECTIVE REBUILDING, RESTORATION, AND RESETTLEMENT PROGRAM EVER UNDERTAKEN BY THE UNITED STATES GOVERNMENT.
JONES
WHAT'S THIS?
ALL AVAILABLE DATA ABOUT THE REFUGEES, THE EXTENT OF THE DESTRUCTION, AND THE RESOURCES AVAILABLE TO US.
WELCOME BACK TO THE HUMAN RACE.
RIGHT...
JONES
TAPPETY TAP TAP TAP
...AND TOMORROW YOU'LL HAVE ME PLOTTING BOMBING RUNS ON THE OVERSEAS ENEMY OF THE DAY.
KID, THAT STUFF HAS NOTHING TO DO WITH--
WHATEVER, DUDE. I READ "ENDER'S GAME."
AND NOW, IF I'M READING THE RIPPLES IN THAT WATER BOWL RIGHT, YOU BETTER DUCK.
WHAT?
S.H.I.E.L.

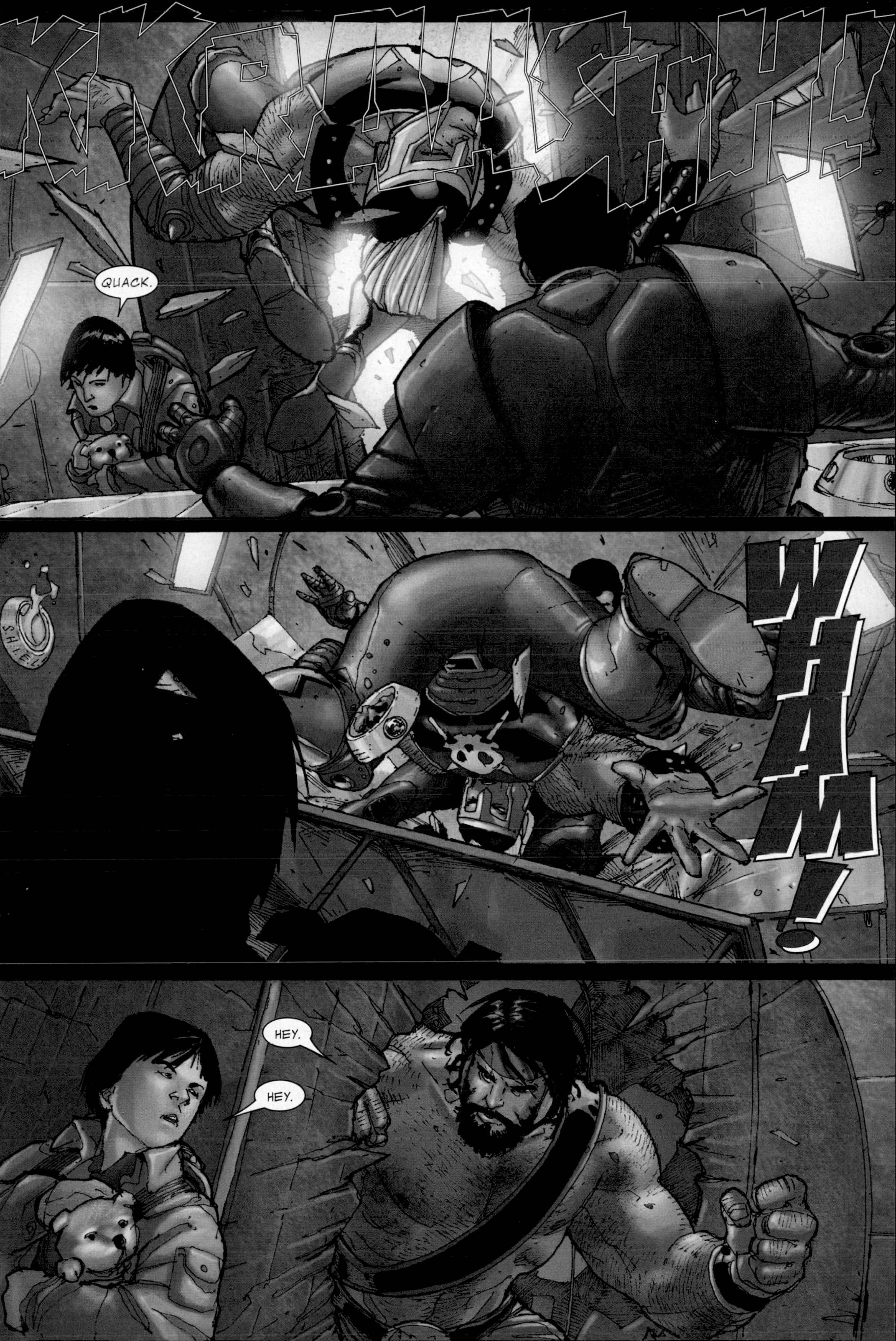
QUACK.
WHAM!
HEY.
HEY.

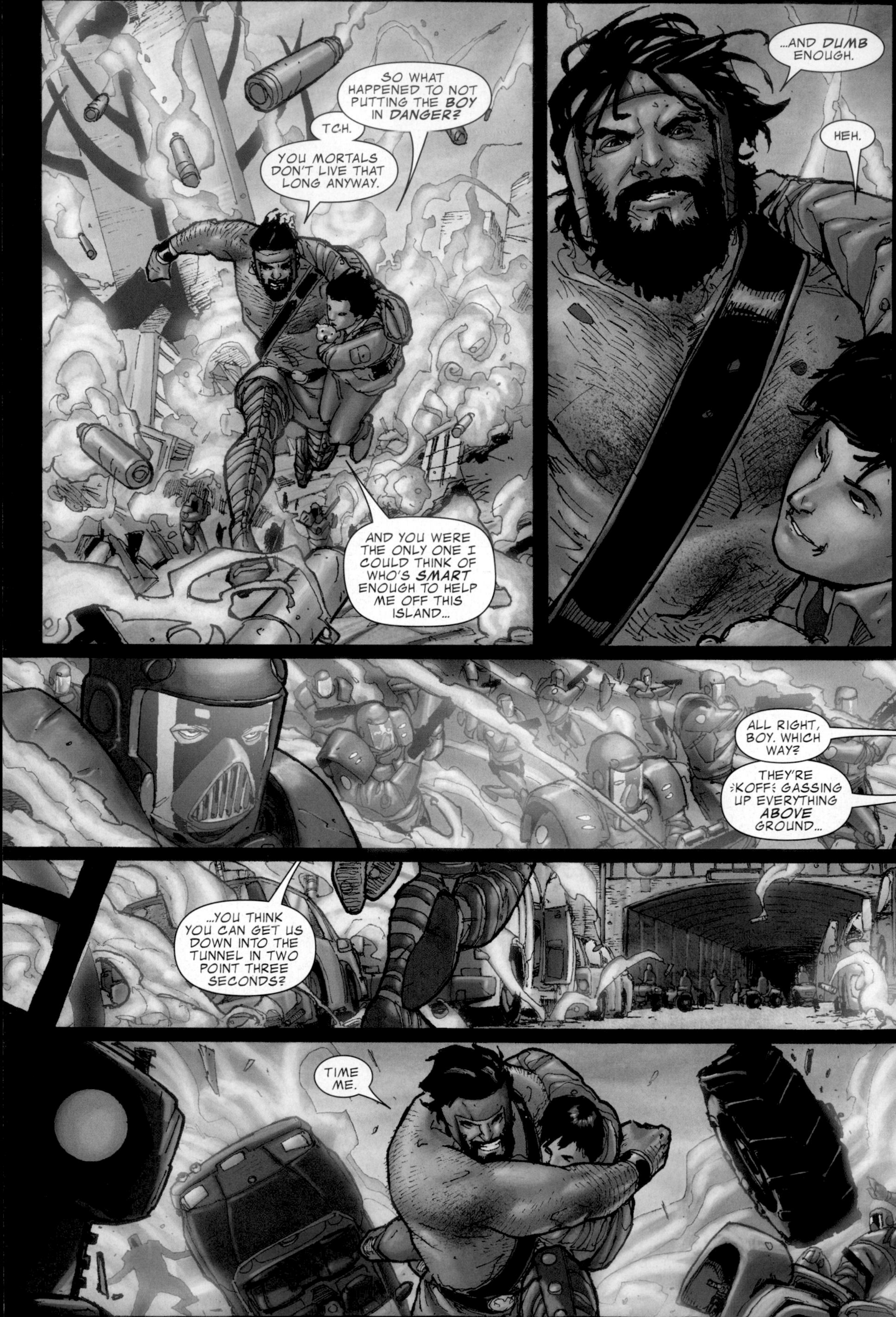
TCH.
YOU MORTALS DON'T LIVE THAT LONG ANYWAY.
SO WHAT HAPPENED TO NOT PUTTING THE BOY IN DANGER?
AND YOU WERE THE ONLY ONE I COULD THINK OF WHO'S SMART ENOUGH TO HELP ME OFF THIS ISLAND...
...AND DUMB ENOUGH.
HEH.
ALL RIGHT, BOY. WHICH WAY?
THEY'RE *KOFF* GASSING UP EVERYTHING ABOVE GROUND...
...YOU THINK YOU CAN GET US DOWN INTO THE TUNNEL IN TWO POINT THREE SECONDS?
TIME ME.

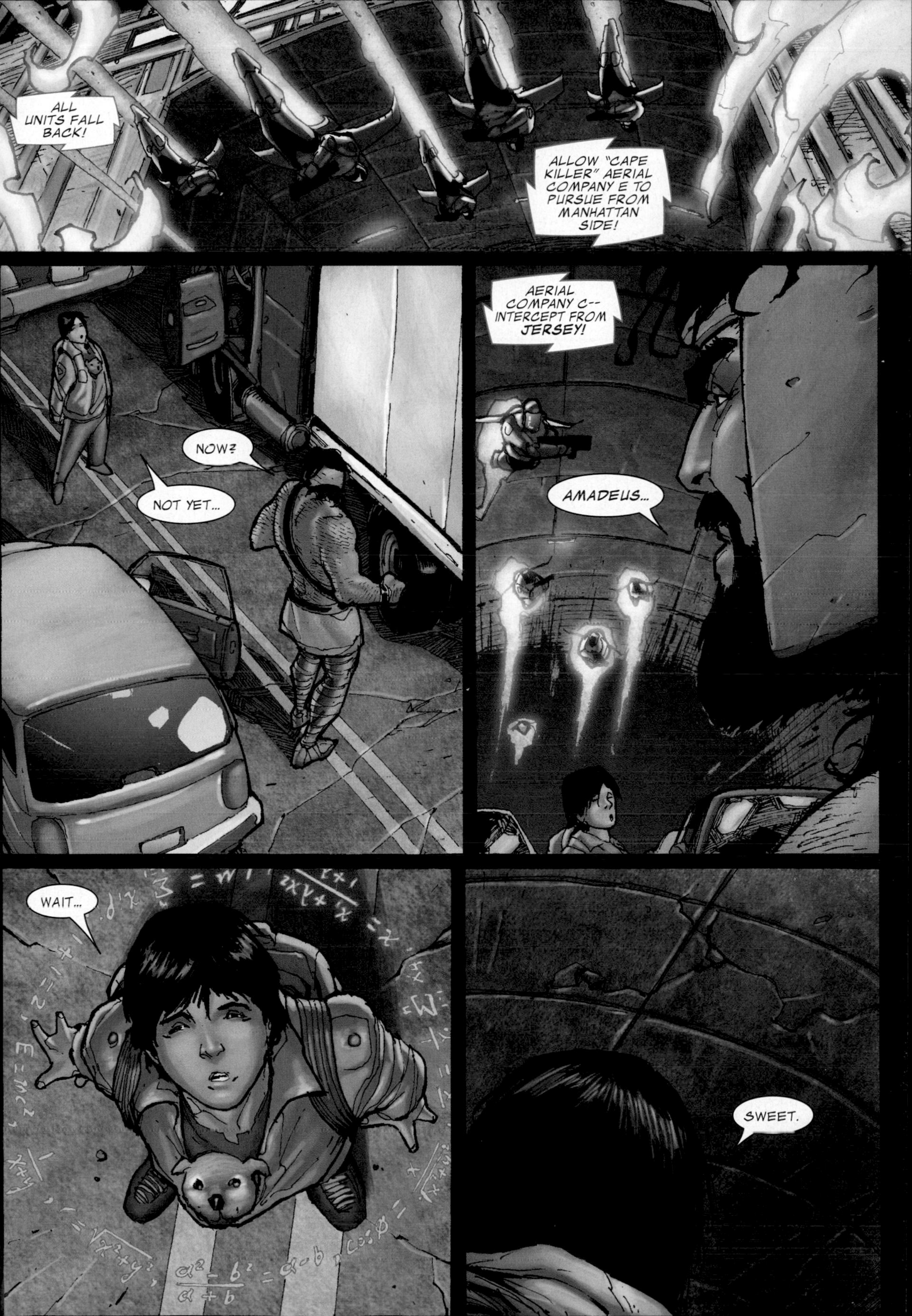
ALL UNITS FALL BACK!
ALLOW "CAPE KILLER" AERIAL COMPANY E TO PURSUE FROM MANHATTAN SIDE!
NOW?
NOT YET...
AERIAL COMPANY C-- INTERCEPT FROM JERSEY!
AMADEUS...
WAIT...
SWEET.

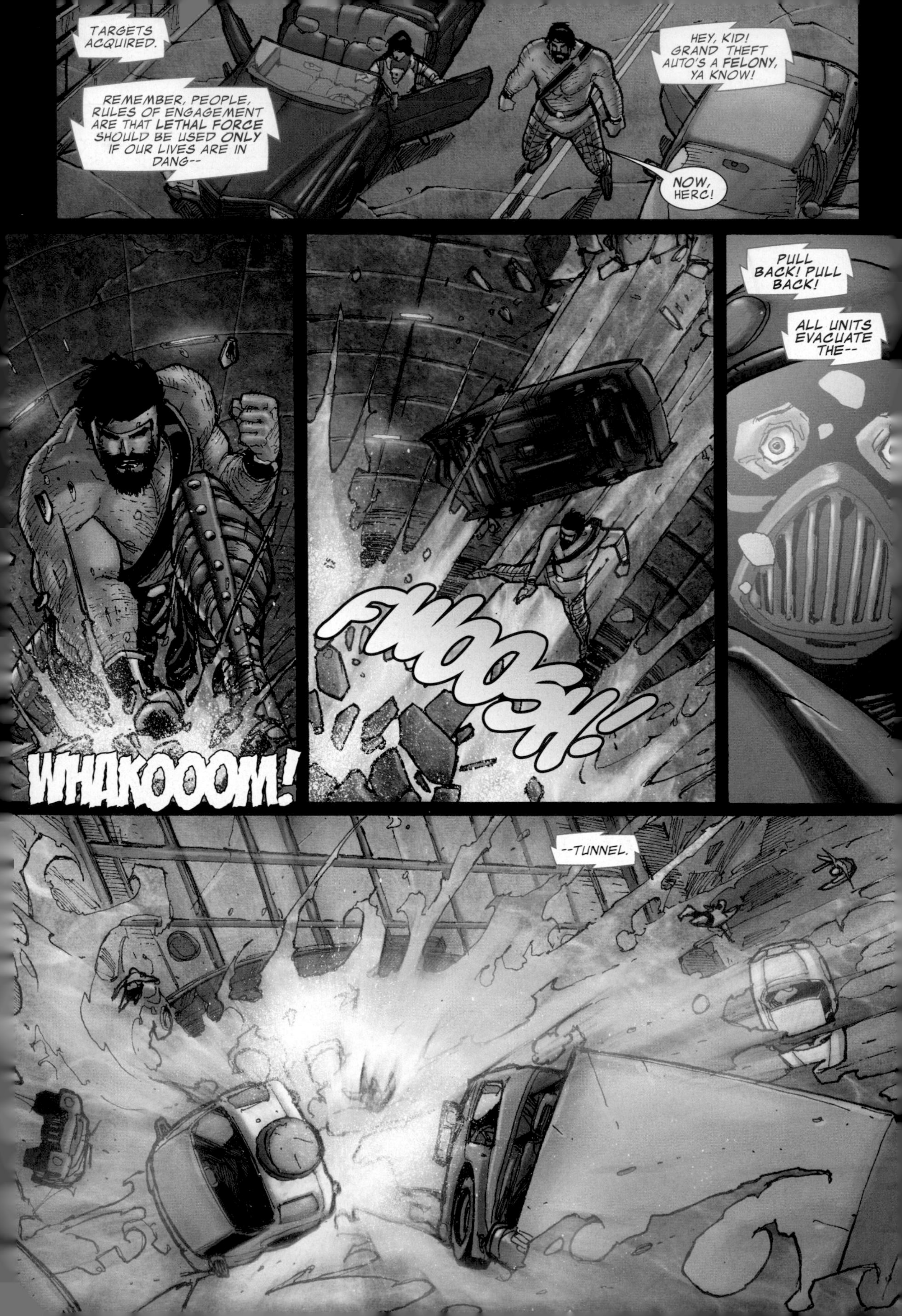
TARGETS ACQUIRED.
REMEMBER, PEOPLE, RULES OF ENGAGEMENT ARE THAT LETHAL FORCE SHOULD BE USED ONLY IF OUR LIVES ARE IN DANG--
HEY, KID! GRAND THEFT AUTO'S A FELONY, YA KNOW!
NOW, HERC!
WHAKOOOM!
FWOOSH!
PULL BACK! PULL BACK!
ALL UNITS EVACUATE THE--
--TUNNEL.

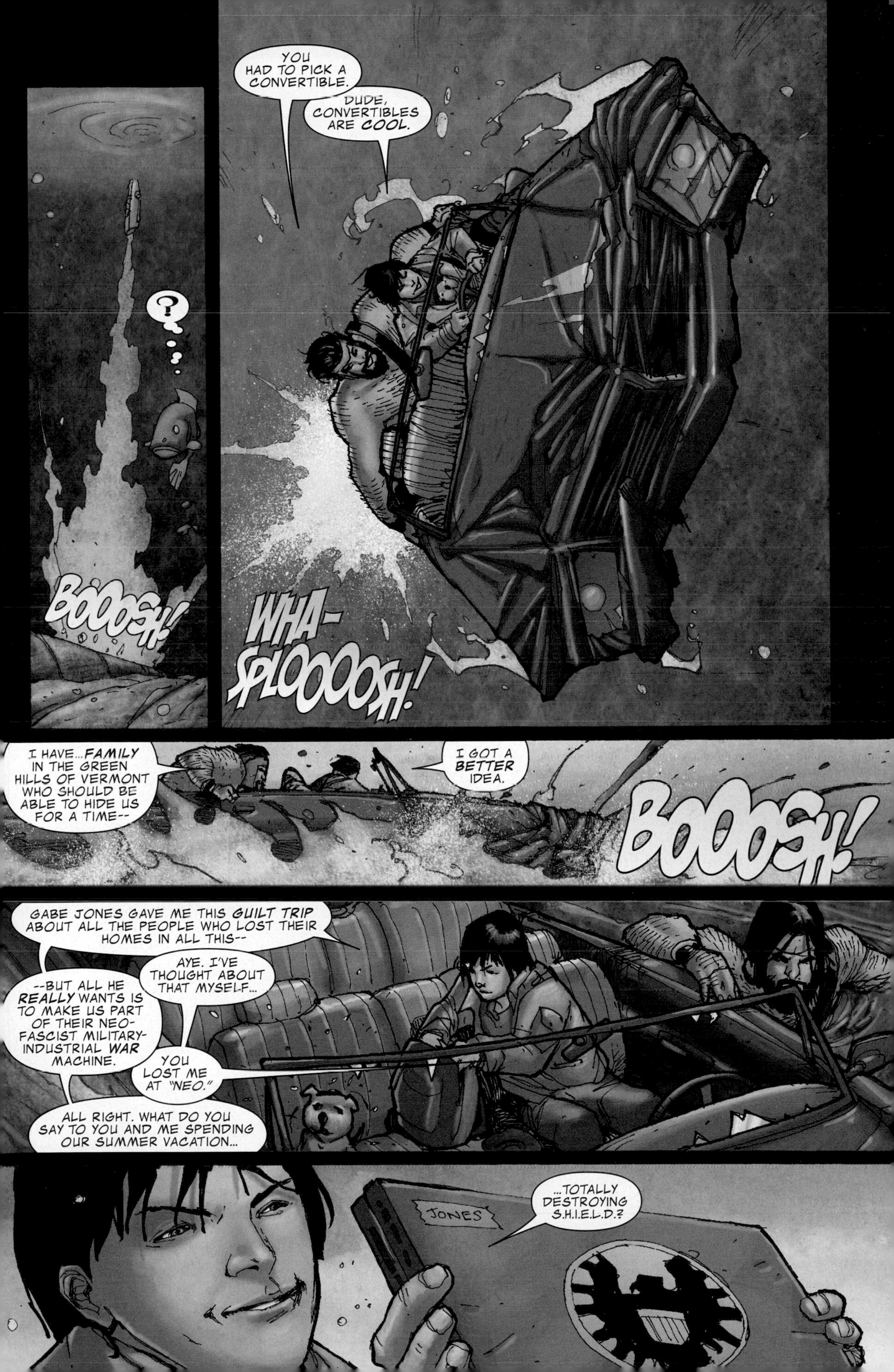

?
BOOOSH!
YOU HAD TO PICK A CONVERTIBLE.
DUDE, CONVERTIBLES ARE COOL.
WHA-SPLOOOOOSH!
I HAVE...FAMILY IN THE GREEN HILLS OF VERMONT WHO SHOULD BE ABLE TO HIDE US FOR A TIME--
I GOT A BETTER IDEA.
BOOOSH!
GABE JONES GAVE ME THIS GUILT TRIP ABOUT ALL THE PEOPLE WHO LOST THEIR HOMES IN ALL THIS--
--BUT ALL HE REALLY WANTS IS TO MAKE US PART OF THEIR NEO-FASCIST MILITARY-INDUSTRIAL WAR MACHINE.
AYE. I'VE THOUGHT ABOUT THAT MYSELF...
YOU LOST ME AT "NEO."
ALL RIGHT. WHAT DO YOU SAY TO YOU AND ME SPENDING OUR SUMMER VACATION...
JONES
...TOTALLY DESTROYING S.H.I.E.L.D.?

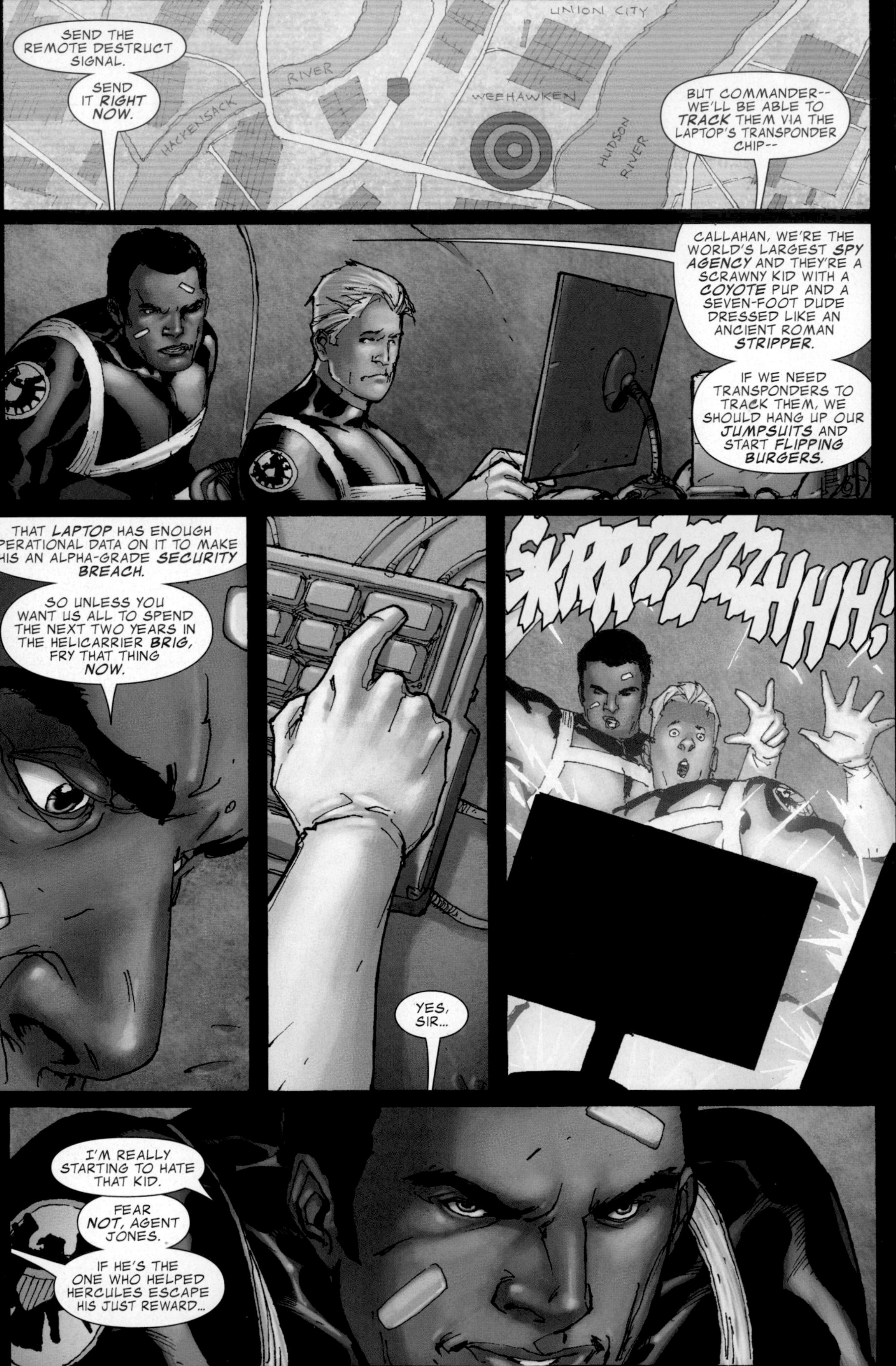

UNION CITY
RIVER
WEEHAWKEN
HACKENSACK
HUDSON RIVER
SEND THE REMOTE DESTRUCT SIGNAL.
SEND IT RIGHT NOW.
BUT COMMANDER-- WE'LL BE ABLE TO TRACK THEM VIA THE LAPTOP'S TRANSPONDER CHIP--
CALLAHAN, WE'RE THE WORLD'S LARGEST SPY AGENCY AND THEY'RE A SCRAWNY KID WITH A COYOTE PUP AND A SEVEN-FOOT DUDE DRESSED LIKE AN ANCIENT ROMAN STRIPPER.
IF WE NEED TRANSPONDERS TO TRACK THEM, WE SHOULD HANG UP OUR JUMPSUITS AND START FLIPPING BURGERS.
THAT LAPTOP HAS ENOUGH OPERATIONAL DATA ON IT TO MAKE THIS AN ALPHA-GRADE SECURITY BREACH.
SO UNLESS YOU WANT US ALL TO SPEND THE NEXT TWO YEARS IN THE HELICARRIER BRIG, FRY THAT THING NOW.
YES, SIR...
SKRRZZZZHHH!
I'M REALLY STARTING TO HATE THAT KID.
FEAR NOT, AGENT JONES.
IF HE'S THE ONE WHO HELPED HERCULES ESCAPE HIS JUST REWARD...

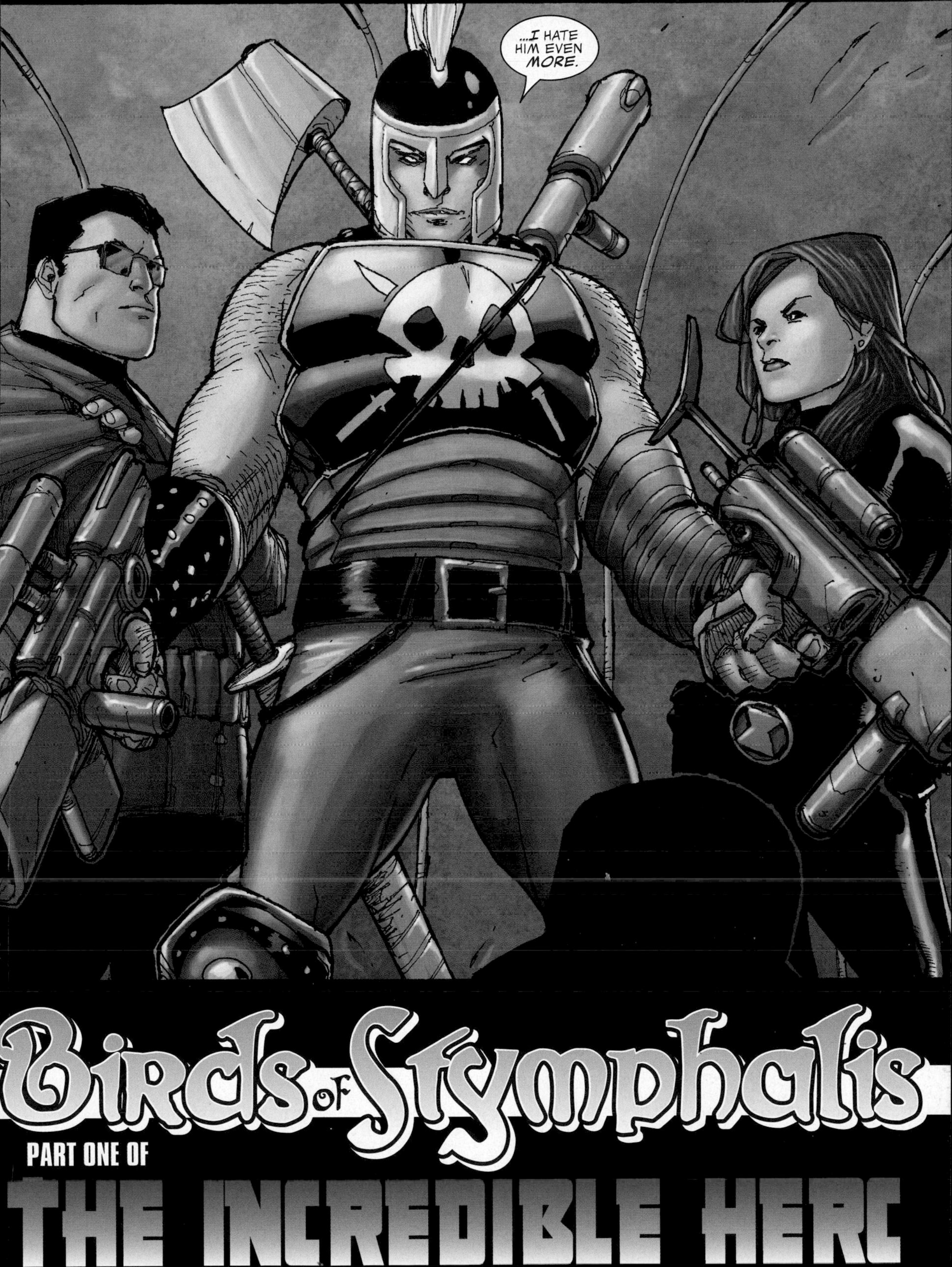
...I HATE HIM EVEN MORE.
Birds of Stymphalis
PART ONE OF
THE INCREDIBLE HERC

Yo. This is Amadeus. Mr. Cho if you're nasty.

And this...is a quiz. I'm waaaaaaaaaay smarter than you, so it'll take you longer to answer than the 26 seconds it took me to come up with the questions.

1) WHAT WAS AMADEUS' SCORE ON THE "BRAIN FIGHT" GAME SHOW?

2) WHAT'D HERCULES KILL GERYON WITH? BE SPECIFIC, YO.

3) HOW MANY WORDS ARE ON THE THIRTY-EIGHTH PAGE OF AMADEUS' SECOND COMIC BOOK APPEARANCE?

4) WHAT DID HERCULES CREATE AFTER HE REROUTED THE ALPHEUS AND PENEUS RIVERS?

5) NAME THREE OF THE SATELLITES THAT SHOT HULK AT THE END OF...AH, SHOOT...WHATEVER THAT RECENT MINISERIES WITH HULK IN IT WAS CALLED.

6) WHO TAUGHT HERCULES TO WRESTLE?

7) AFTER HERC BEAT THE CRAP OUT OF ARES THE SECOND TIME, WHO THREW ARES IN A CHARIOT AND TOOK HIM TO OLYMPUS?

8) WHAT'S THE NAME OF THE CRAFT THAT I BOUGHT WITH WORTHINGTON'S MONEY?

9) HOW MANY DAUGHTERS DID HERC HAVE WITH DEÏANEIRA? NAMES, PLEASE.

10) WHO WROTE A SONG ABOUT THE STRAIT THAT HERCULES CREATED?

10. ALEXANDER GORODNITSKY
9. ONE (MACARIA)
8. M-43 COSBY AMPHIBIOUS FLYER
7. DEIMUS (FEAR) AND PHOBUS (PANIC)
6. AUTOLYCUS
5. CHINESE FIRESTARS, SHI'AR, RUSSIAN
4. THE OLYMPIC GAMES
3. 296 (297 GIVES YOU A BONUS POINT)
2. OLIVE-WOOD CLUB
1. 7,839

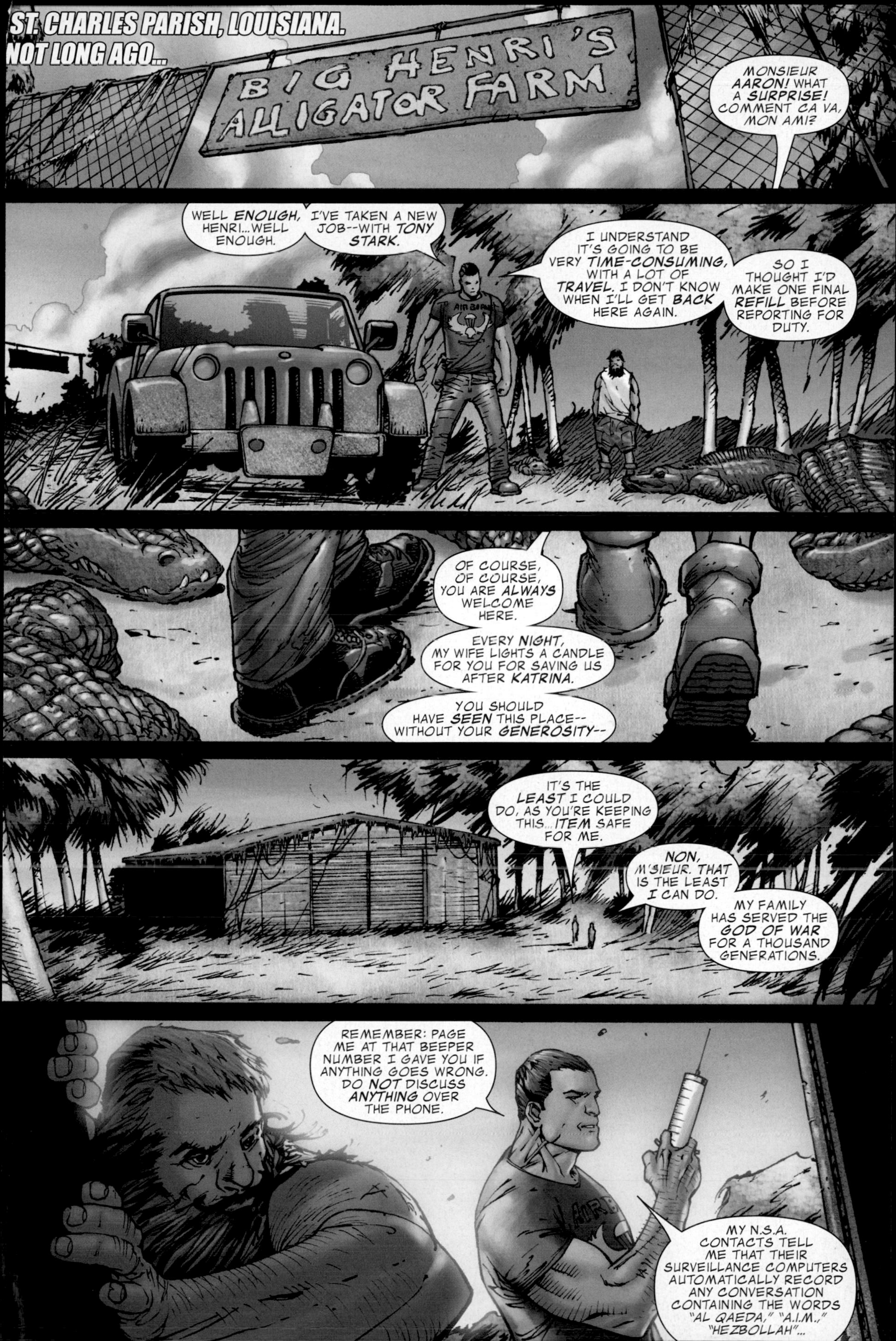
ST. CHARLES PARISH, LOUISIANA. NOT LONG AGO...
BIG HENRI'S ALLIGATOR FARM
MONSIEUR AARON! WHAT A SURPRISE! COMMENT CA VA, MON AMI?
WELL ENOUGH, HENRI...WELL ENOUGH.
I'VE TAKEN A NEW JOB--WITH TONY STARK.
I UNDERSTAND IT'S GOING TO BE VERY TIME-CONSUMING, WITH A LOT OF TRAVEL. I DON'T KNOW WHEN I'LL GET BACK HERE AGAIN.
SO I THOUGHT I'D MAKE ONE FINAL REFILL BEFORE REPORTING FOR DUTY.
OF COURSE, OF COURSE, YOU ARE ALWAYS WELCOME HERE.
EVERY NIGHT, MY WIFE LIGHTS A CANDLE FOR YOU FOR SAVING US AFTER KATRINA.
YOU SHOULD HAVE SEEN THIS PLACE--WITHOUT YOUR GENEROSITY--
IT'S THE LEAST I COULD DO, AS YOU'RE KEEPING THIS...ITEM SAFE FOR ME.
NON, M'SIEUR. THAT IS THE LEAST I CAN DO.
MY FAMILY HAS SERVED THE GOD OF WAR FOR A THOUSAND GENERATIONS.
REMEMBER: PAGE ME AT THAT BEEPER NUMBER I GAVE YOU IF ANYTHING GOES WRONG. DO NOT DISCUSS ANYTHING OVER THE PHONE.
MY N.S.A. CONTACTS TELL ME THAT THEIR SURVEILLANCE COMPUTERS AUTOMATICALLY RECORD ANY CONVERSATION CONTAINING THE WORDS "AL QAEDA," "A.I.M.," "HEZBOLLAH"...

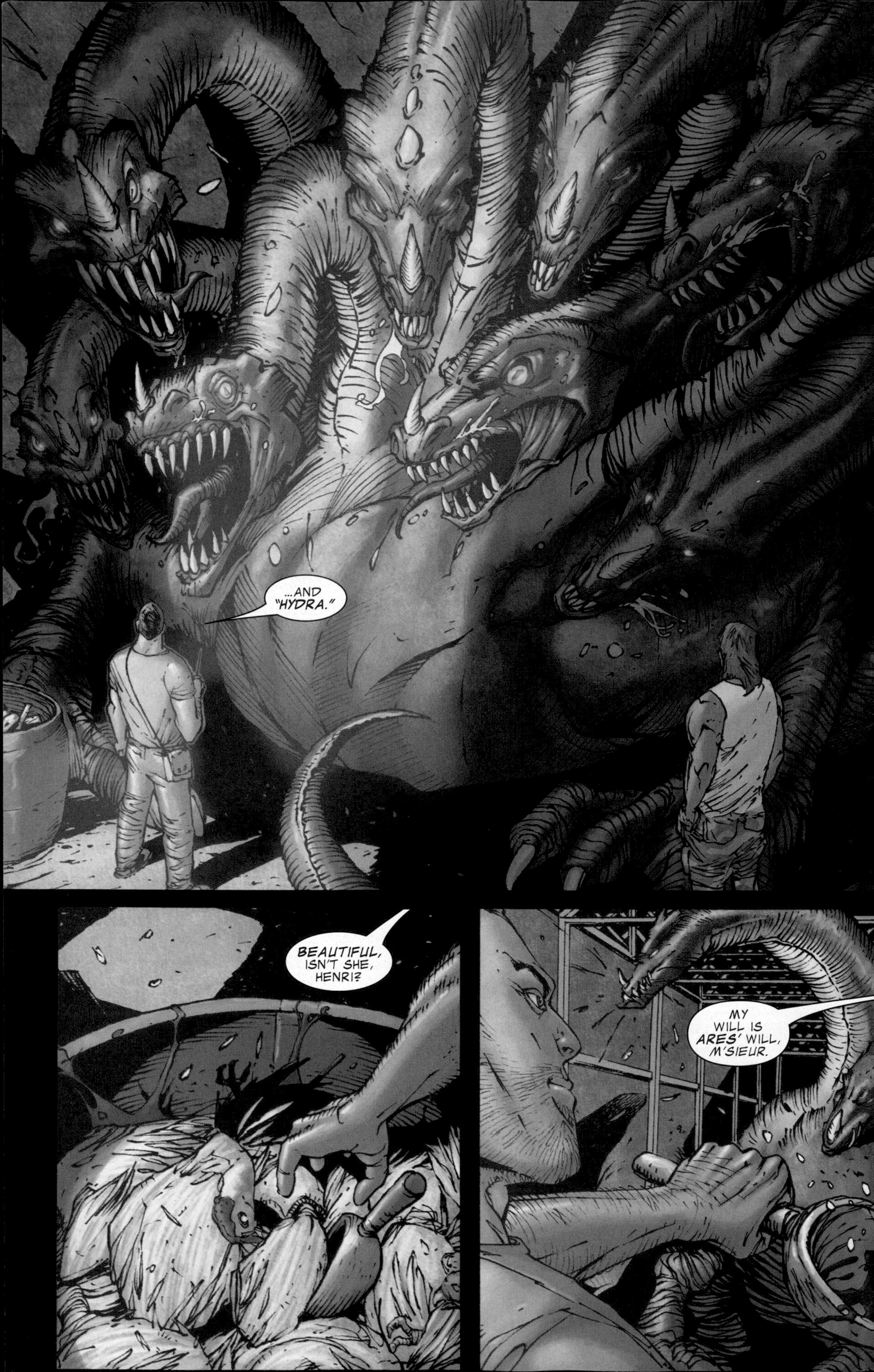
...AND "HYDRA."
BEAUTIFUL, ISN'T SHE, HENRI?
MY WILL IS ARES' WILL, M'SIEUR.

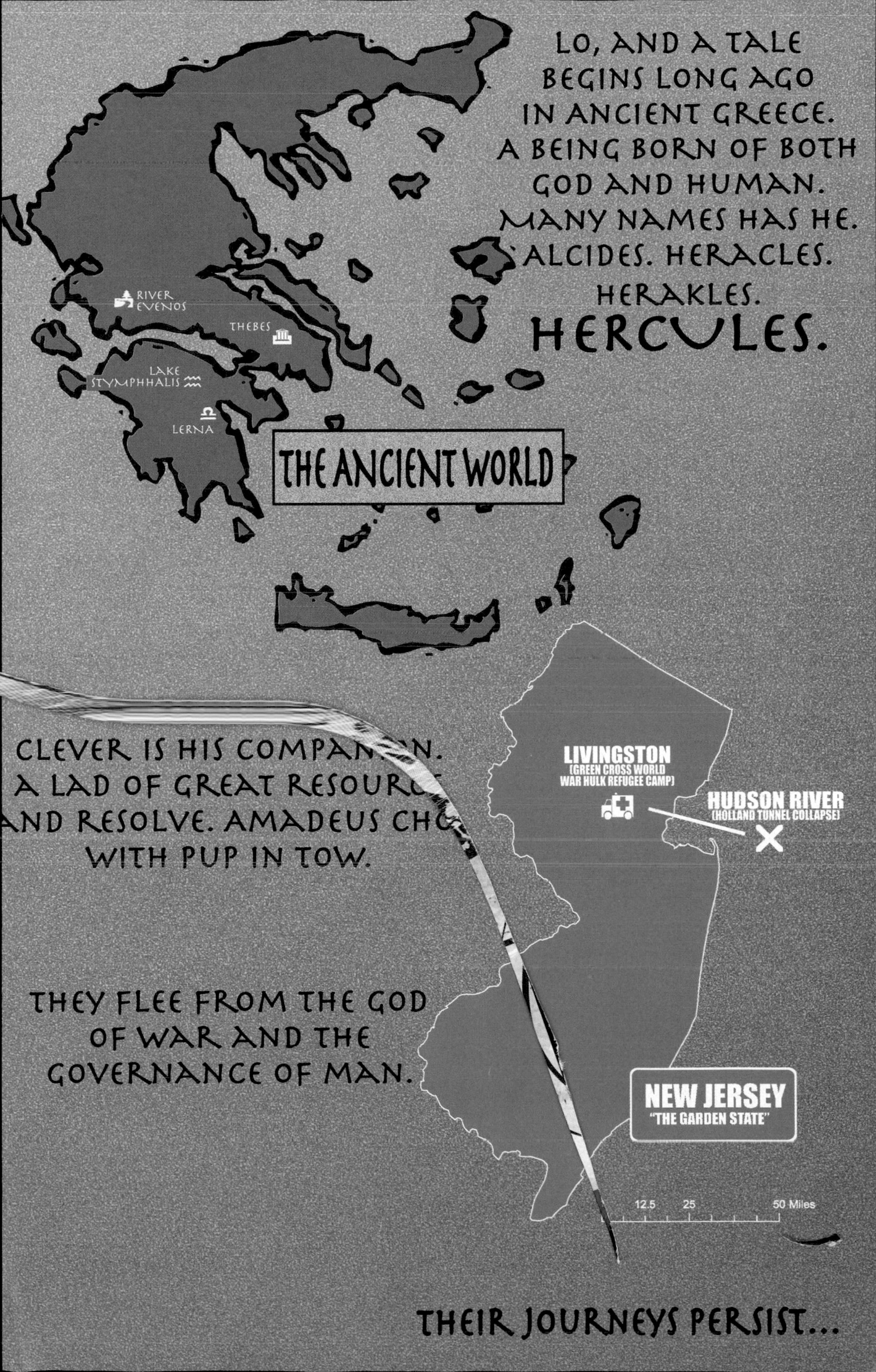

LO, AND A TALE
BEGINS LONG AGO
IN ANCIENT GREECE.
A BEING BORN OF BOTH
GOD AND HUMAN.
MANY NAMES HAS HE.
ALCIDES. HERACLES.
HERAKLES.

HERCULES.

RIVER
EVENOS

THEBES

LAKE
STYMPHHALIS

LERNA

THE ANCIENT WORLD

CLEVER IS HIS COMPANION.
A LAD OF GREAT RESOURCE
AND RESOLVE. AMADEUS CHO
WITH PUP IN TOW.

LIVINGSTON
(GREEN CROSS WORLD
WAR HULK REFUGEE CAMP)

HUDSON RIVER
(HOLLAND TUNNEL COLLAPSE)

THEY FLEE FROM THE GOD
OF WAR AND THE
GOVERNANCE OF MAN.

NEW JERSEY
"THE GARDEN STATE"

12.5   25   50 Miles

THEIR JOURNEYS PERSIST...

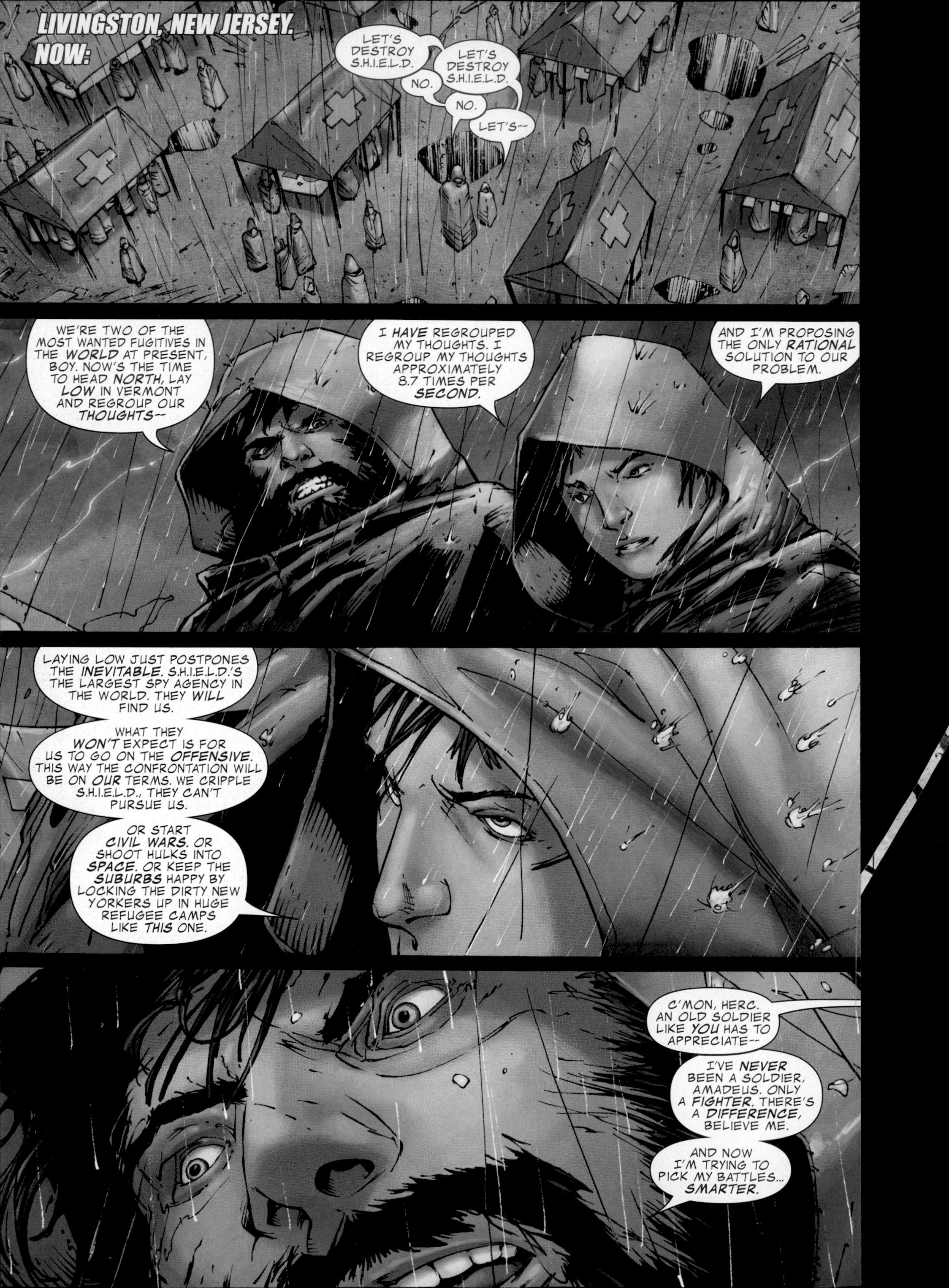
LIVINGSTON, NEW JERSEY. NOW:
LET'S DESTROY S.H.I.E.L.D.
LET'S DESTROY S.H.I.E.L.D.
NO.
NO.
LET'S--
WE'RE TWO OF THE MOST WANTED FUGITIVES IN THE WORLD AT PRESENT, BOY. NOW'S THE TIME TO HEAD NORTH, LAY LOW IN VERMONT AND REGROUP OUR THOUGHTS--
I HAVE REGROUPED MY THOUGHTS. I REGROUP MY THOUGHTS APPROXIMATELY 8.7 TIMES PER SECOND.
AND I'M PROPOSING THE ONLY RATIONAL SOLUTION TO OUR PROBLEM.
LAYING LOW JUST POSTPONES THE INEVITABLE. S.H.I.E.L.D.'S THE LARGEST SPY AGENCY IN THE WORLD. THEY WILL FIND US.
WHAT THEY WON'T EXPECT IS FOR US TO GO ON THE OFFENSIVE. THIS WAY THE CONFRONTATION WILL BE ON OUR TERMS. WE CRIPPLE S.H.I.E.L.D., THEY CAN'T PURSUE US.
OR START CIVIL WARS. OR SHOOT HULKS INTO SPACE. OR KEEP THE SUBURBS HAPPY BY LOCKING THE DIRTY NEW YORKERS UP IN HUGE REFUGEE CAMPS LIKE THIS ONE.
C'MON, HERC. AN OLD SOLDIER LIKE YOU HAS TO APPRECIATE--
I'VE NEVER BEEN A SOLDIER, AMADEUS. ONLY A FIGHTER. THERE'S A DIFFERENCE, BELIEVE ME.
AND NOW I'M TRYING TO PICK MY BATTLES... SMARTER.

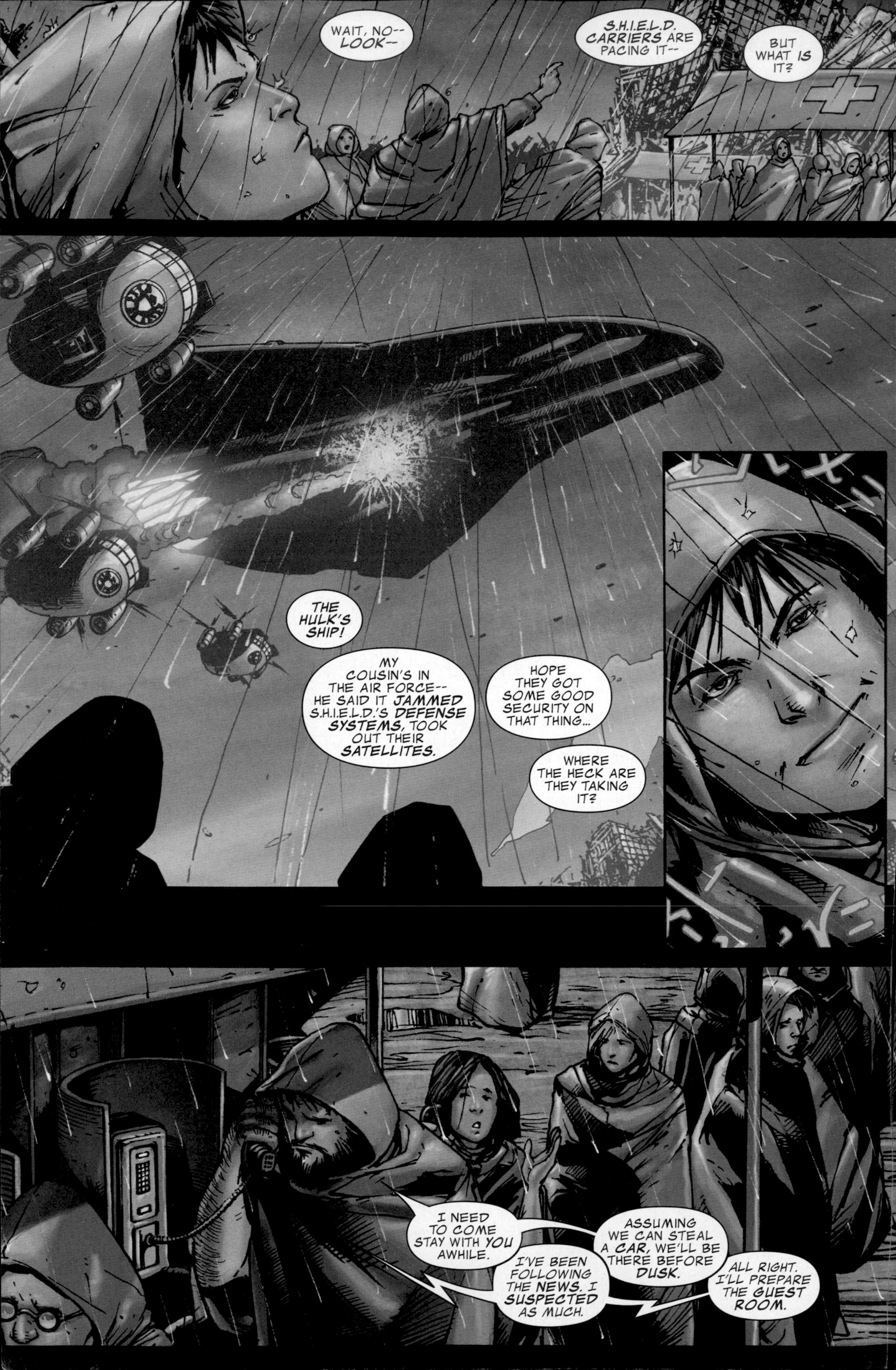
WAIT, NO--
LOOK--
S.H.I.E.L.D. CARRIERS ARE PACING IT--
BUT WHAT IS IT?
THE HULK'S SHIP!
MY COUSIN'S IN THE AIR FORCE-- HE SAID IT JAMMED S.H.I.E.L.D.'S DEFENSE SYSTEMS, TOOK OUT THEIR SATELLITES.
HOPE THEY GOT SOME GOOD SECURITY ON THAT THING...
WHERE THE HECK ARE THEY TAKING IT?
I NEED TO COME STAY WITH YOU AWHILE.
I'VE BEEN FOLLOWING THE NEWS. I SUSPECTED AS MUCH.
ASSUMING WE CAN STEAL A CAR, WE'LL BE THERE BEFORE DUSK.
ALL RIGHT. I'LL PREPARE THE GUEST ROOM.

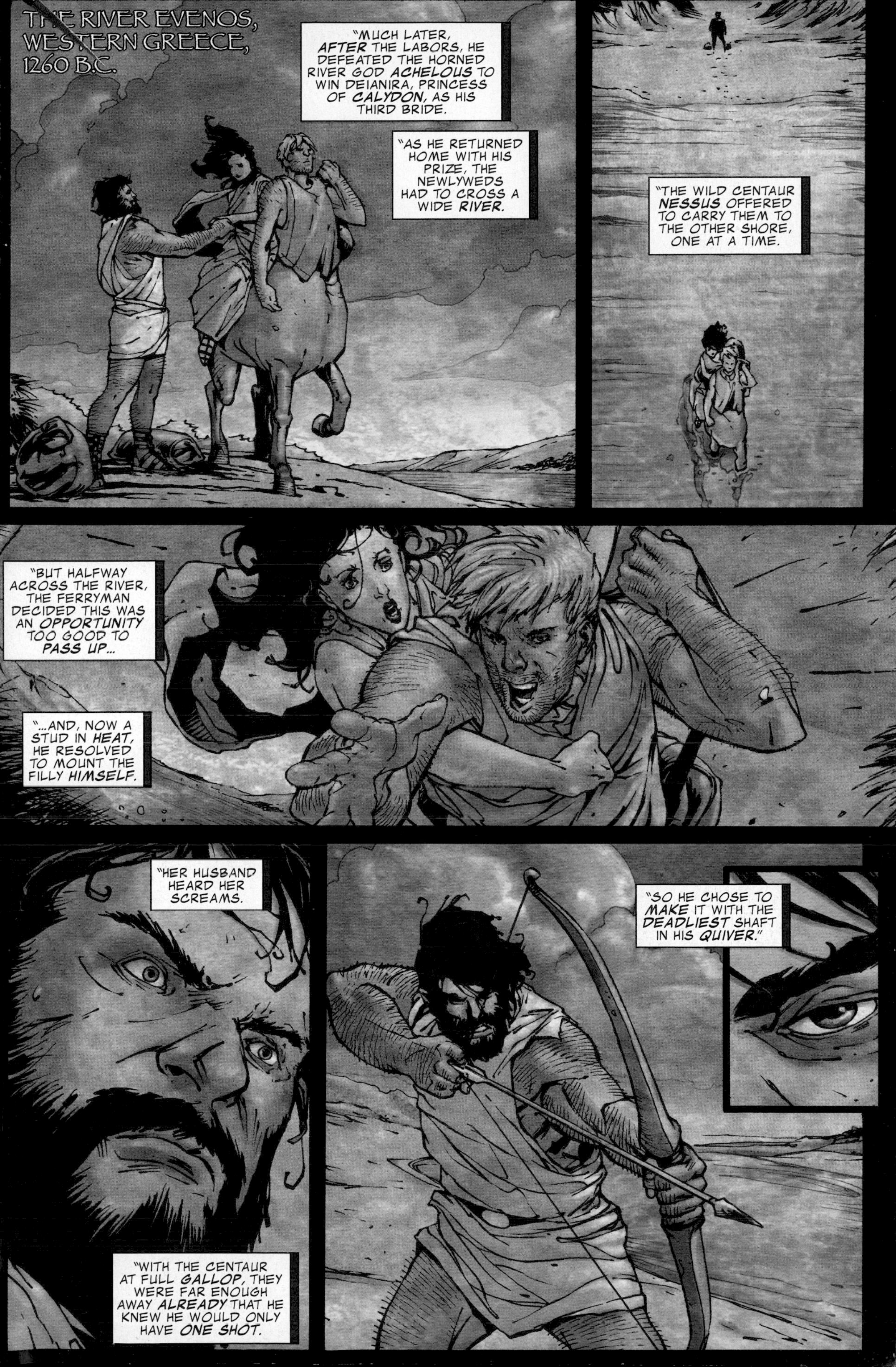
THE RIVER EVENOS, WESTERN GREECE, 1260 B.C.
"MUCH LATER, AFTER THE LABORS, HE DEFEATED THE HORNED RIVER GOD ACHELOUS TO WIN DEIANIRA, PRINCESS OF CALYDON, AS HIS THIRD BRIDE.
"AS HE RETURNED HOME WITH HIS PRIZE, THE NEWLYWEDS HAD TO CROSS A WIDE RIVER.
"THE WILD CENTAUR NESSUS OFFERED TO CARRY THEM TO THE OTHER SHORE, ONE AT A TIME.
"BUT HALFWAY ACROSS THE RIVER, THE FERRYMAN DECIDED THIS WAS AN OPPORTUNITY TOO GOOD TO PASS UP...
"...AND, NOW A STUD IN HEAT, HE RESOLVED TO MOUNT THE FILLY HIMSELF.
"HER HUSBAND HEARD HER SCREAMS.
"WITH THE CENTAUR AT FULL GALLOP, THEY WERE FAR ENOUGH AWAY ALREADY THAT HE KNEW HE WOULD ONLY HAVE ONE SHOT.
"SO HE CHOSE TO MAKE IT WITH THE DEADLIEST SHAFT IN HIS QUIVER."

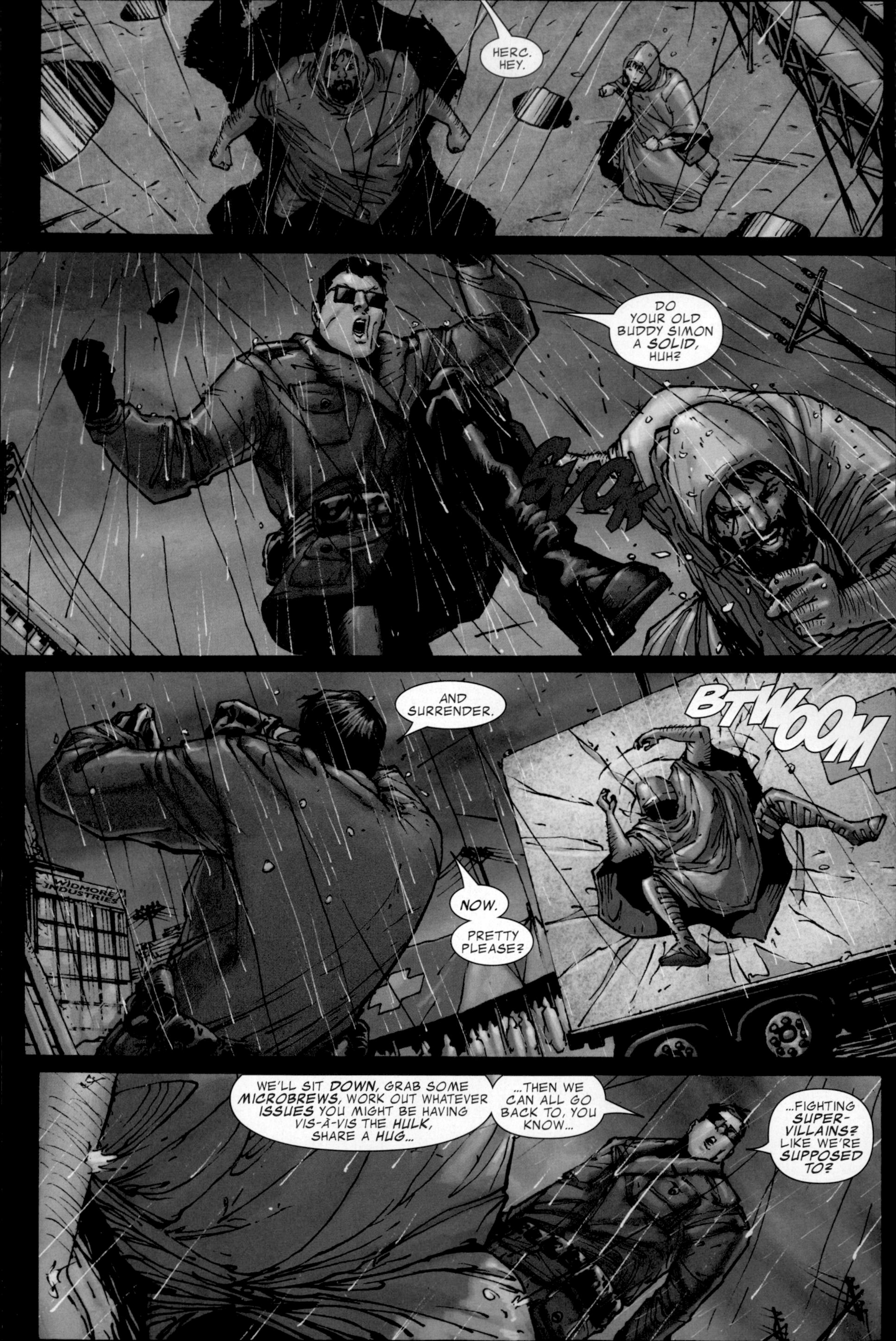
HERC. HEY.
DO YOUR OLD BUDDY SIMON A SOLID, HUH?
SVOK
AND SURRENDER.
BTWOOM
NOW.
PRETTY PLEASE?
WIDMORE INDUSTRIES
WE'LL SIT DOWN, GRAB SOME MICROBREWS, WORK OUT WHATEVER ISSUES YOU MIGHT BE HAVING VIS-Á-VIS THE HULK, SHARE A HUG...
...THEN WE CAN ALL GO BACK TO, YOU KNOW...
...FIGHTING SUPER-VILLAINS? LIKE WE'RE SUPPOSED TO?

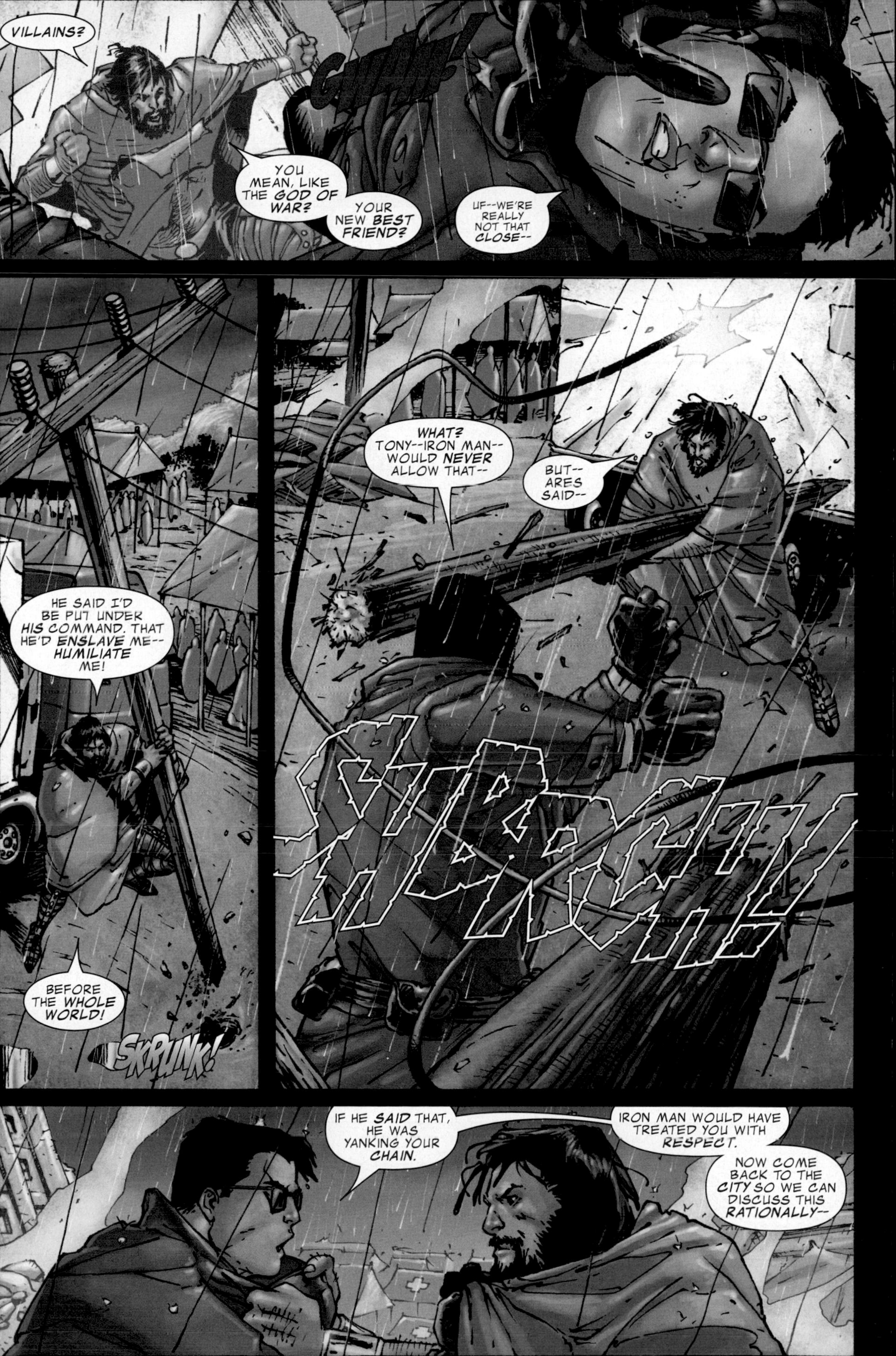
VILLAINS?
YOU MEAN, LIKE THE GOD OF WAR?
YOUR NEW BEST FRIEND?
UF--WE'RE REALLY NOT THAT CLOSE--
WHAT? TONY--IRON MAN--WOULD NEVER ALLOW THAT--
BUT--ARES SAID--
HE SAID I'D BE PUT UNDER HIS COMMAND. THAT HE'D ENSLAVE ME--HUMILIATE ME!
BEFORE THE WHOLE WORLD!
SKRUNK!
IF HE SAID THAT, HE WAS YANKING YOUR CHAIN.
IRON MAN WOULD HAVE TREATED YOU WITH RESPECT.
NOW COME BACK TO THE CITY SO WE CAN DISCUSS THIS RATIONALLY--

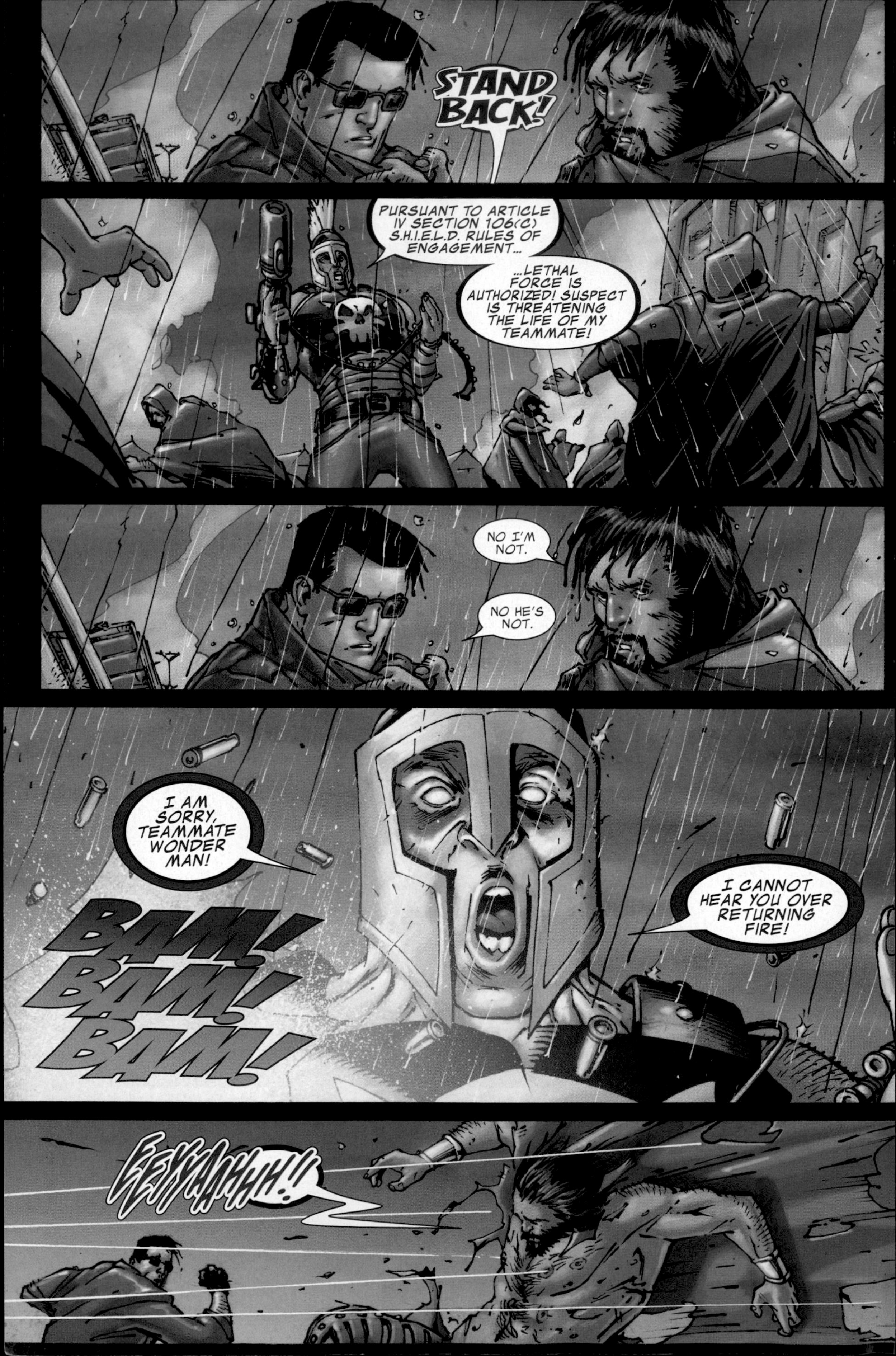
STAND BACK!
PURSUANT TO ARTICLE IV SECTION 106(C) S.H.I.E.L.D. RULES OF ENGAGEMENT...
...LETHAL FORCE IS AUTHORIZED! SUSPECT IS THREATENING THE LIFE OF MY TEAMMATE!
NO I'M NOT.
NO HE'S NOT.
I AM SORRY, TEAMMATE WONDER MAN!
I CANNOT HEAR YOU OVER RETURNING FIRE!
BAM! BAM! BAM!
EEYYAAHHH!!

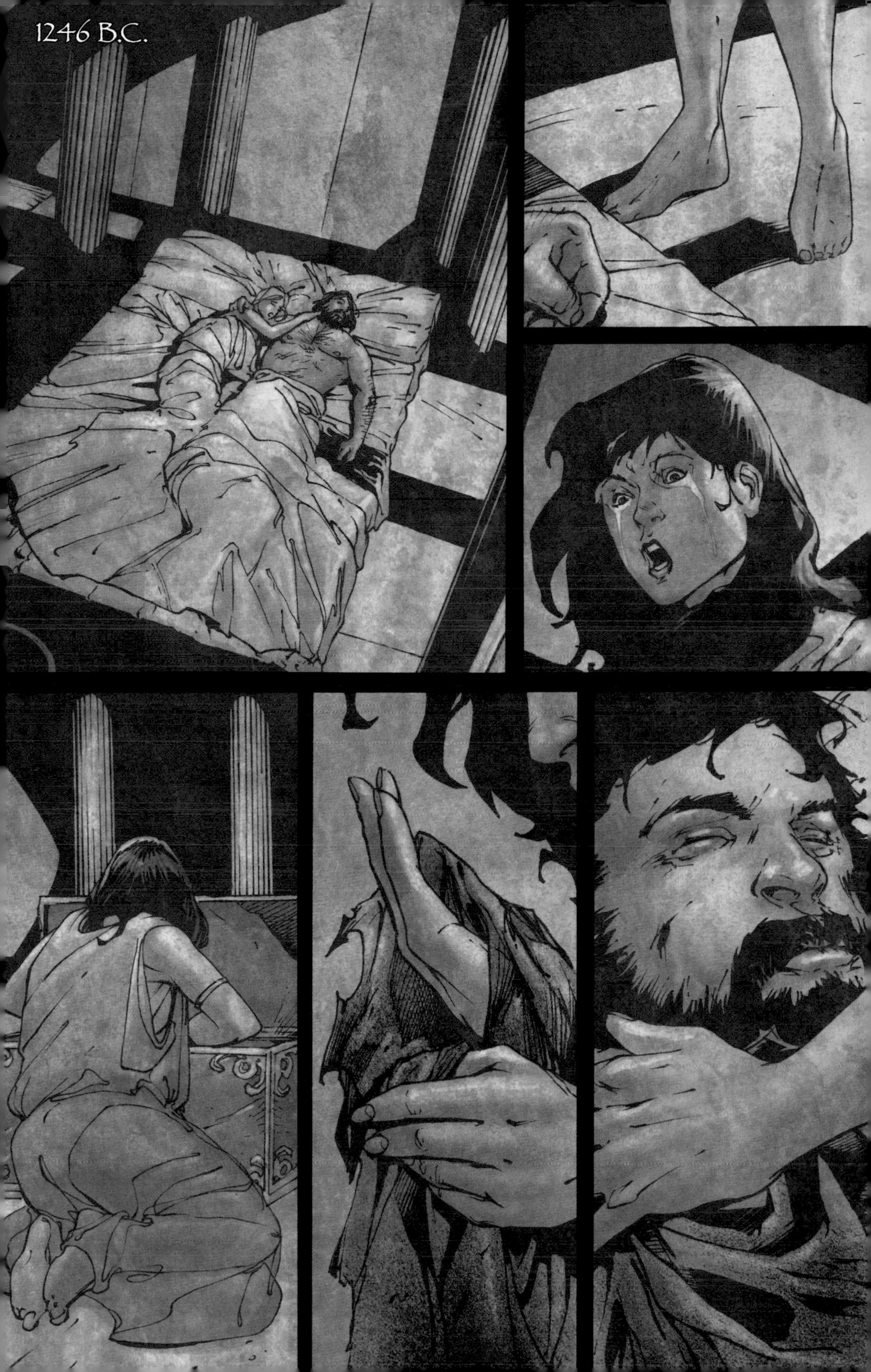
1246 B.C.

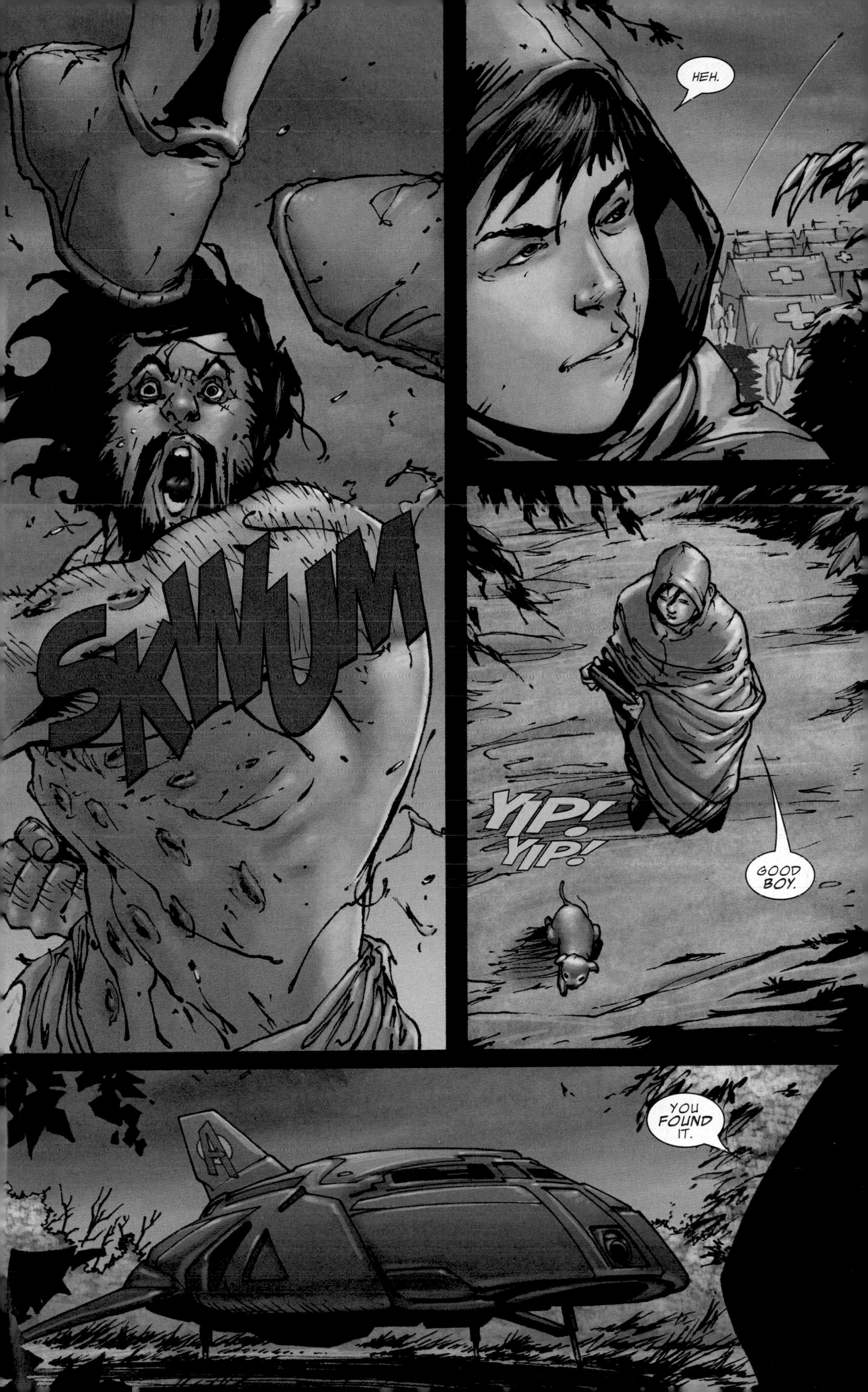
SKWUM
HEH.
YIP! YIP!
GOOD BOY.
YOU FOUND IT.

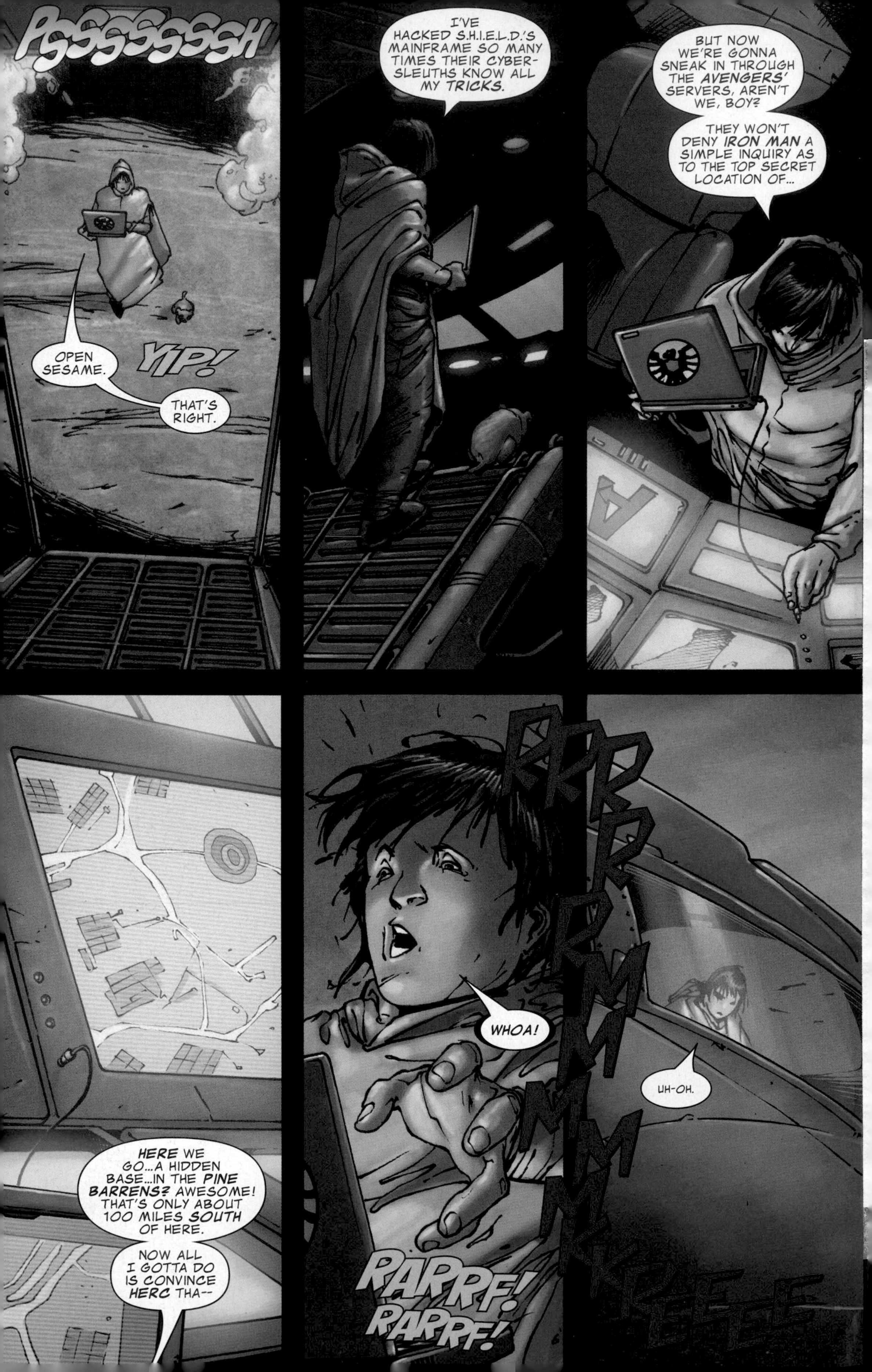
PSSSSSSSH
OPEN SESAME.
YIP!
THAT'S RIGHT.
I'VE HACKED S.H.I.E.L.D.'S MAINFRAME SO MANY TIMES THEIR CYBER-SLEUTHS KNOW ALL MY TRICKS.
BUT NOW WE'RE GONNA SNEAK IN THROUGH THE AVENGERS' SERVERS, AREN'T WE, BOY?
THEY WON'T DENY IRON MAN A SIMPLE INQUIRY AS TO THE TOP SECRET LOCATION OF...
HERE WE GO...A HIDDEN BASE...IN THE PINE BARRENS? AWESOME! THAT'S ONLY ABOUT 100 MILES SOUTH OF HERE.
NOW ALL I GOTTA DO IS CONVINCE HERC THA--
WHOA!
UH-OH.
RARRF! RARRF!

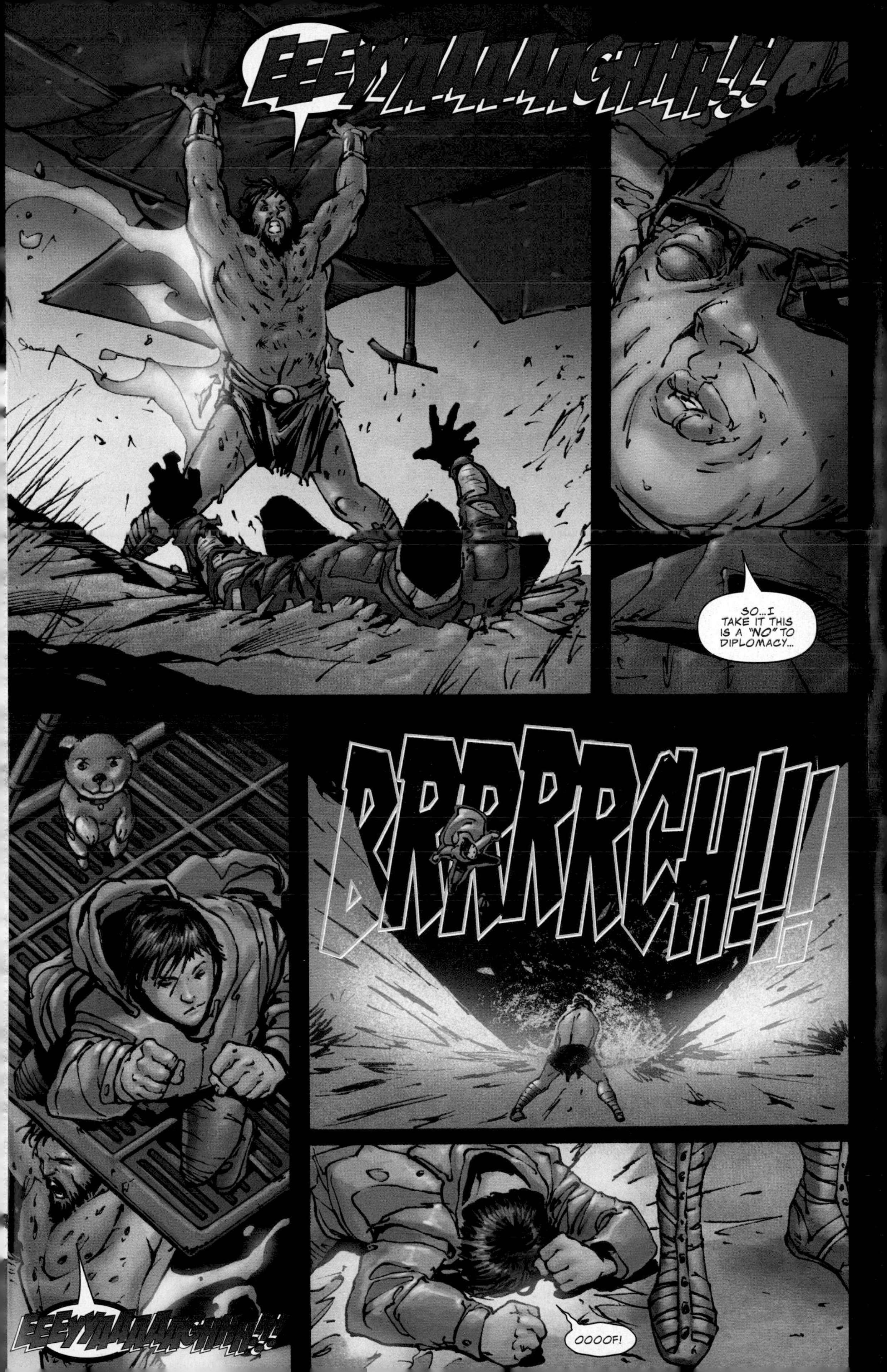

EEEYAAAAAAGHHH!!
SO...I TAKE IT THIS IS A "NO" TO DIPLOMACY...
BRRRRCH!!!
EEEYAAAAAGHHH!!
OOOOF!

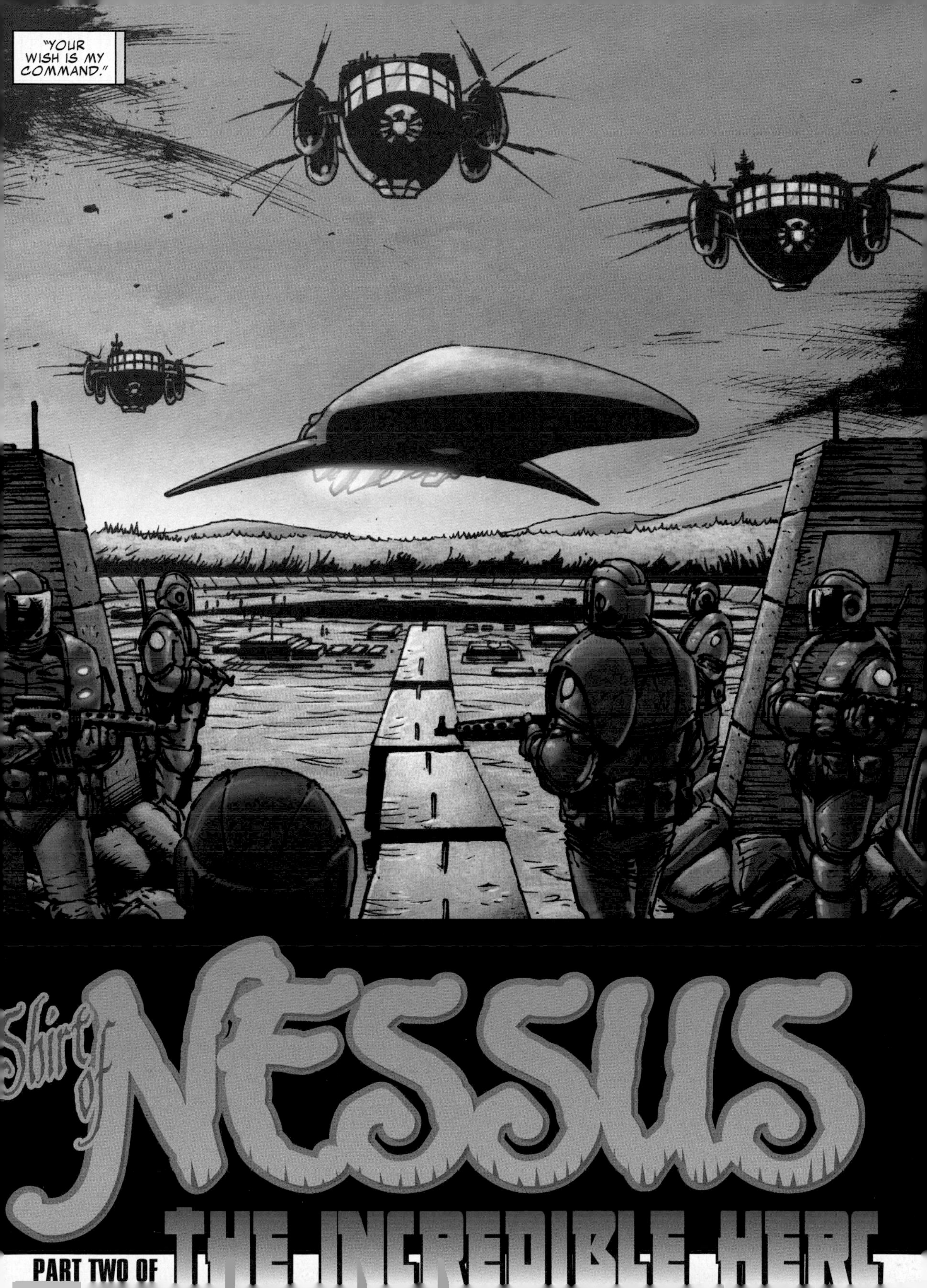
"YOUR WISH IS MY COMMAND."
Shirt of NESSUS
PART TWO OF THE INCREDIBLE HERC

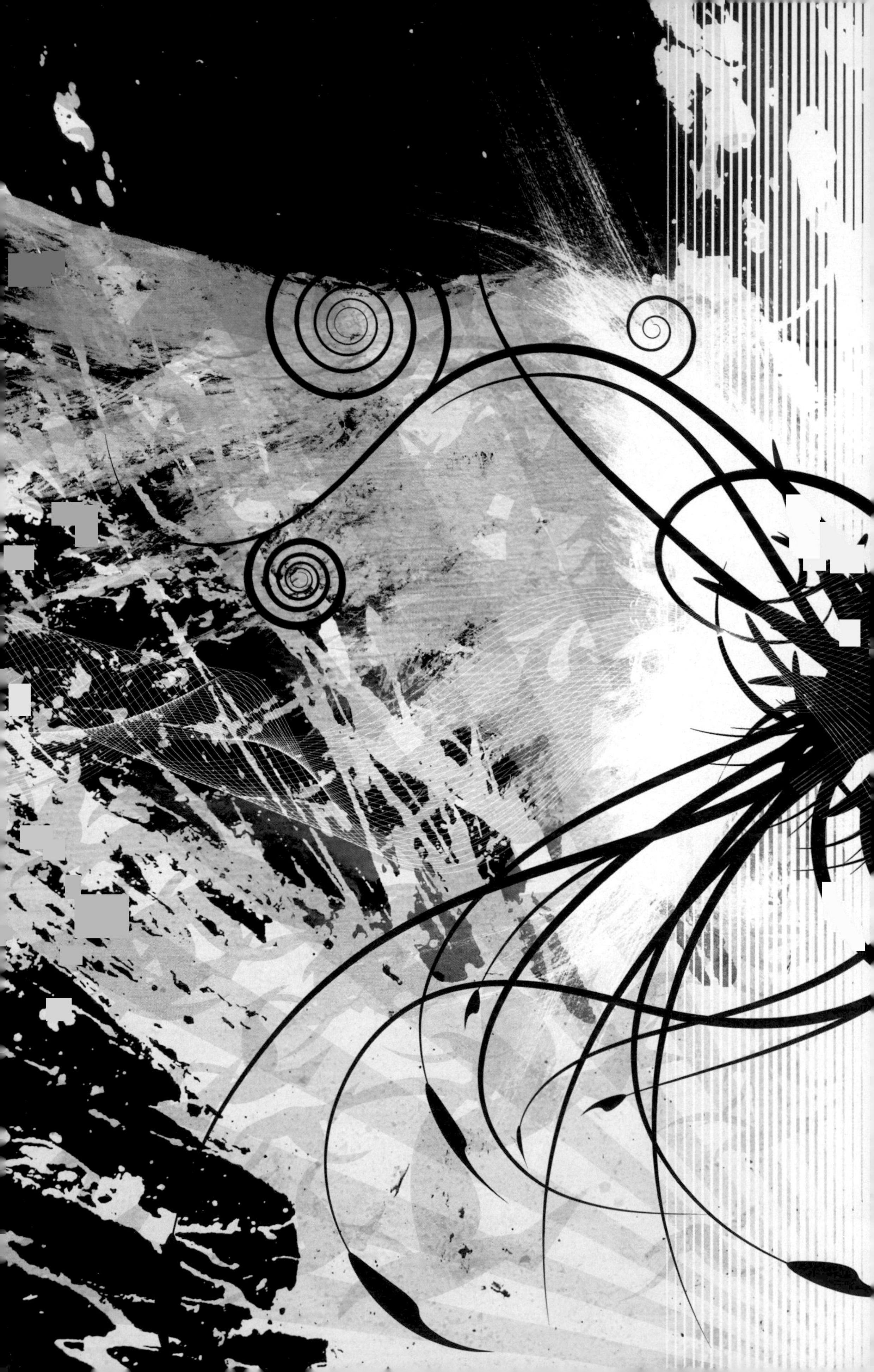

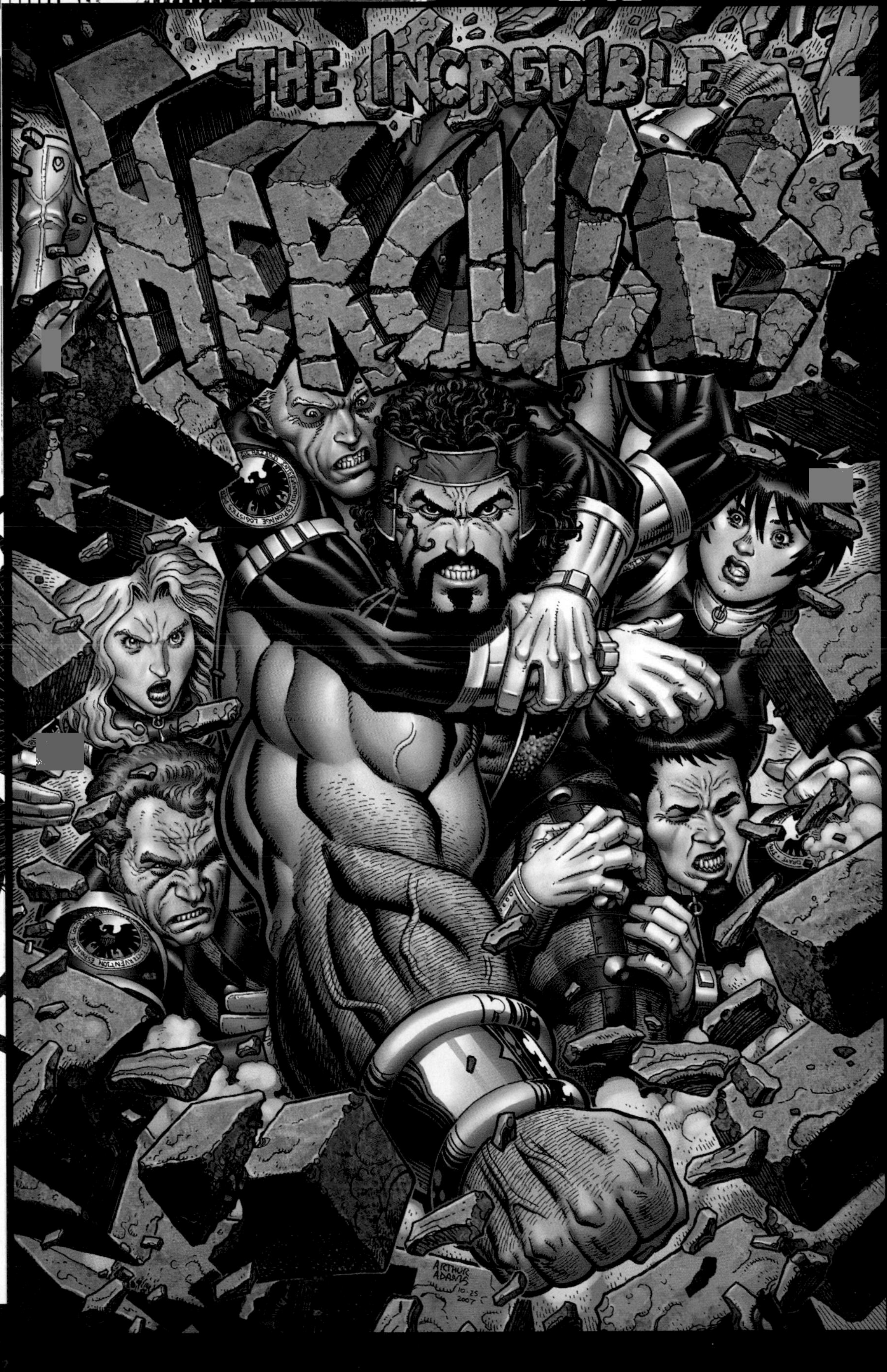
THE INCREDIBLE
HERCULES
ARTHUR ADAMS
10-25 2007

INCREDIBLE HERCULES #114

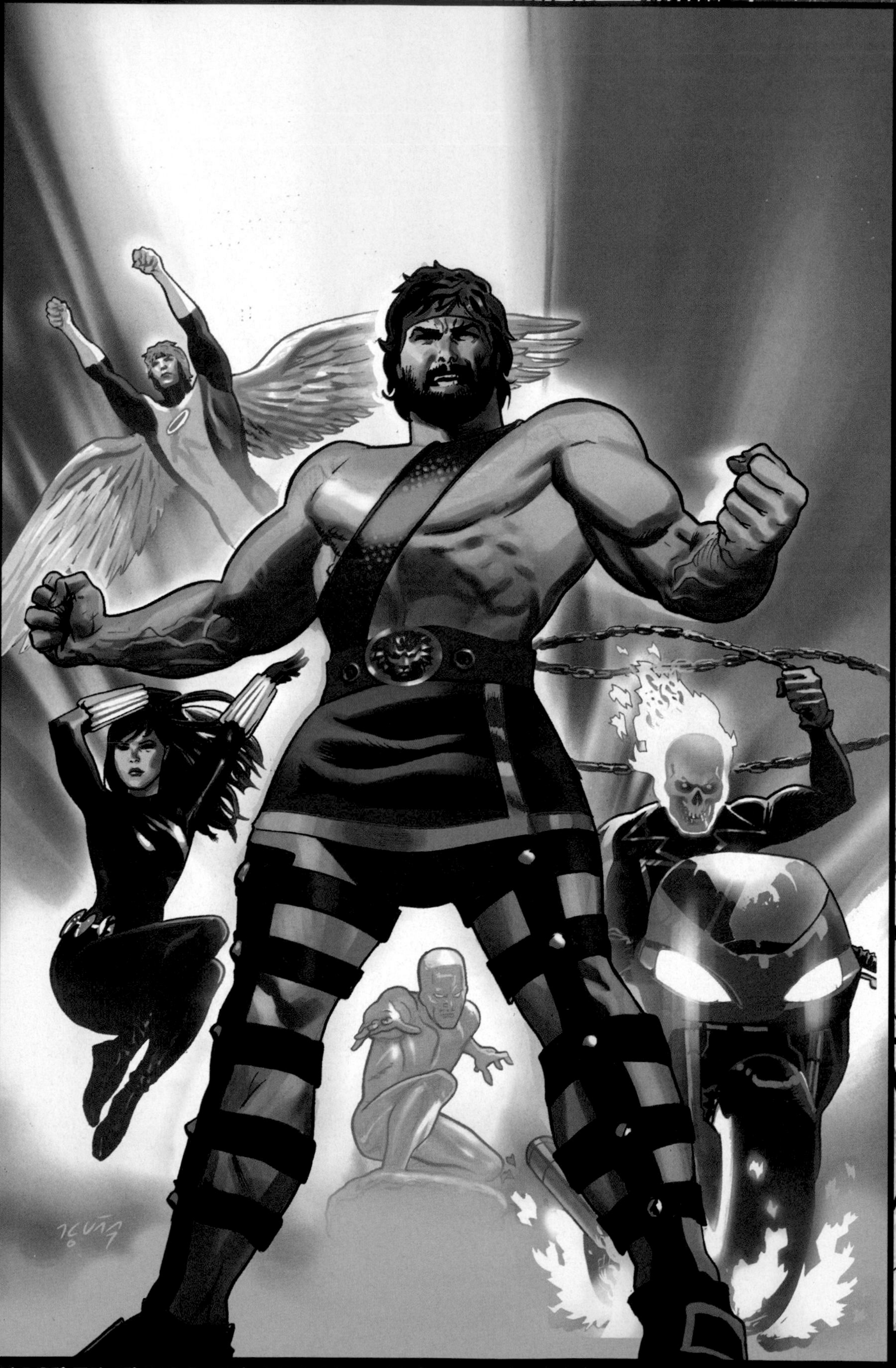

INCREDIBLE HERCULES #114 VARIANT
BY DANIEL ACUÑA

BEHOLD HERCULES.

ARRRRGHH!!!

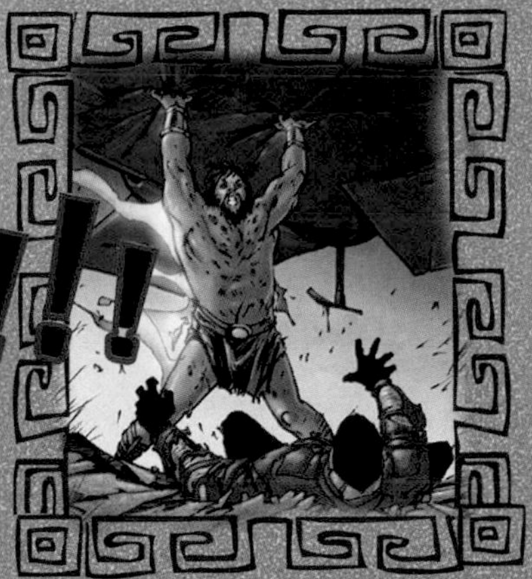

HE'S...ANGRY.

HIS BROTHER, ARES, DIDST SHOOT HIM UP WITH HYDRA BLOOD.

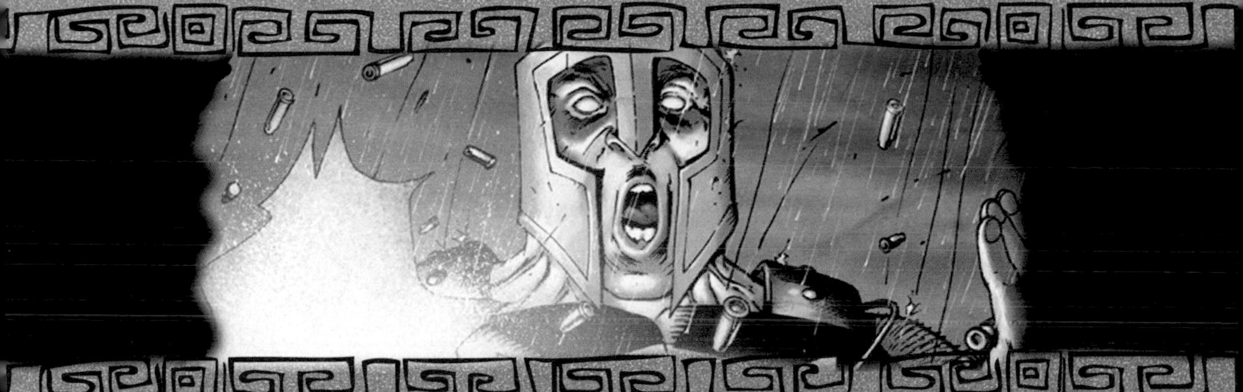

HYDRA BLOOD DOTH DO WONKY THINGS TO HERC.

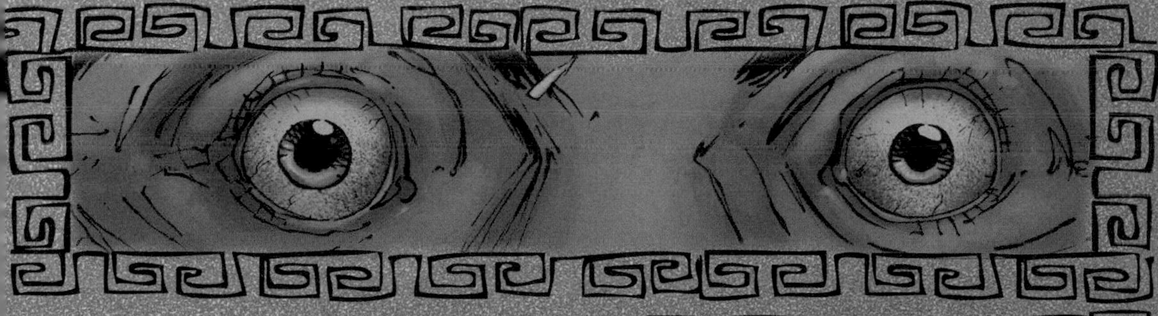

SO WHILST **AMADEUS CHO** (WITH PUP IN TOW) ATTEMPTS TO STEAL YON SHIP OF STONE... →

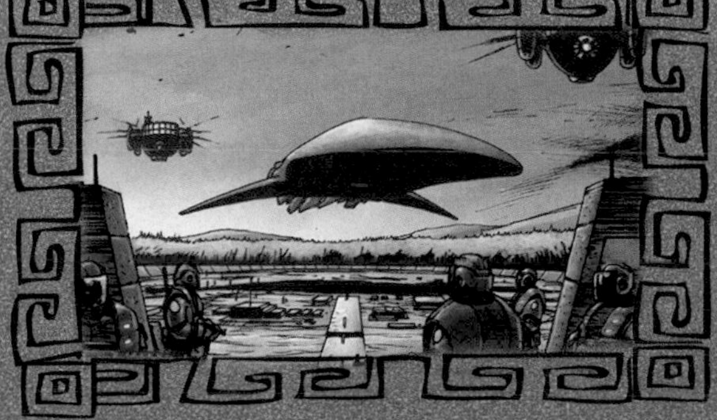

...HERC'S BEATING THE HOLY-LIVING SNOT OUT OF ANYONE HE CAN FIND...

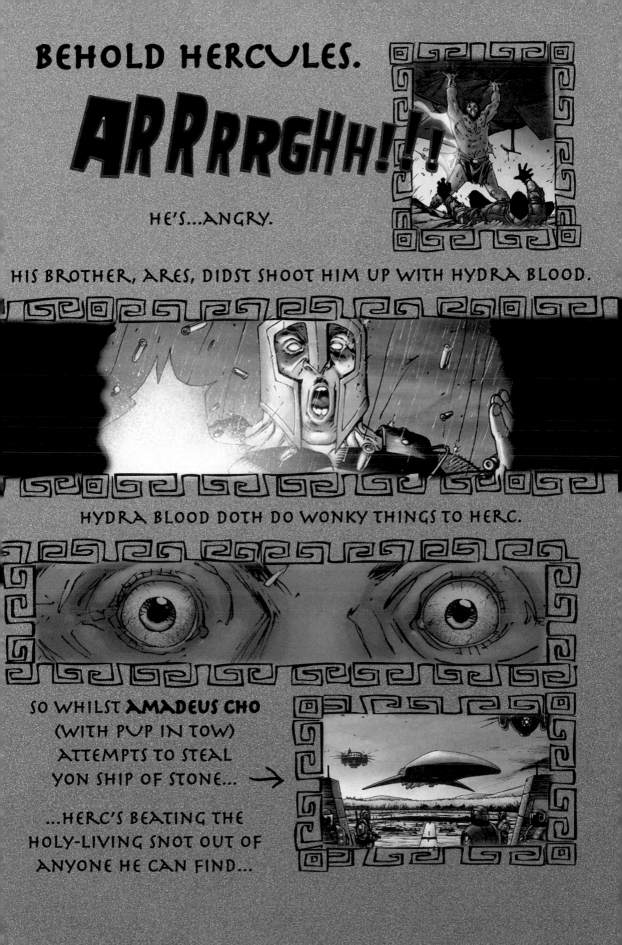

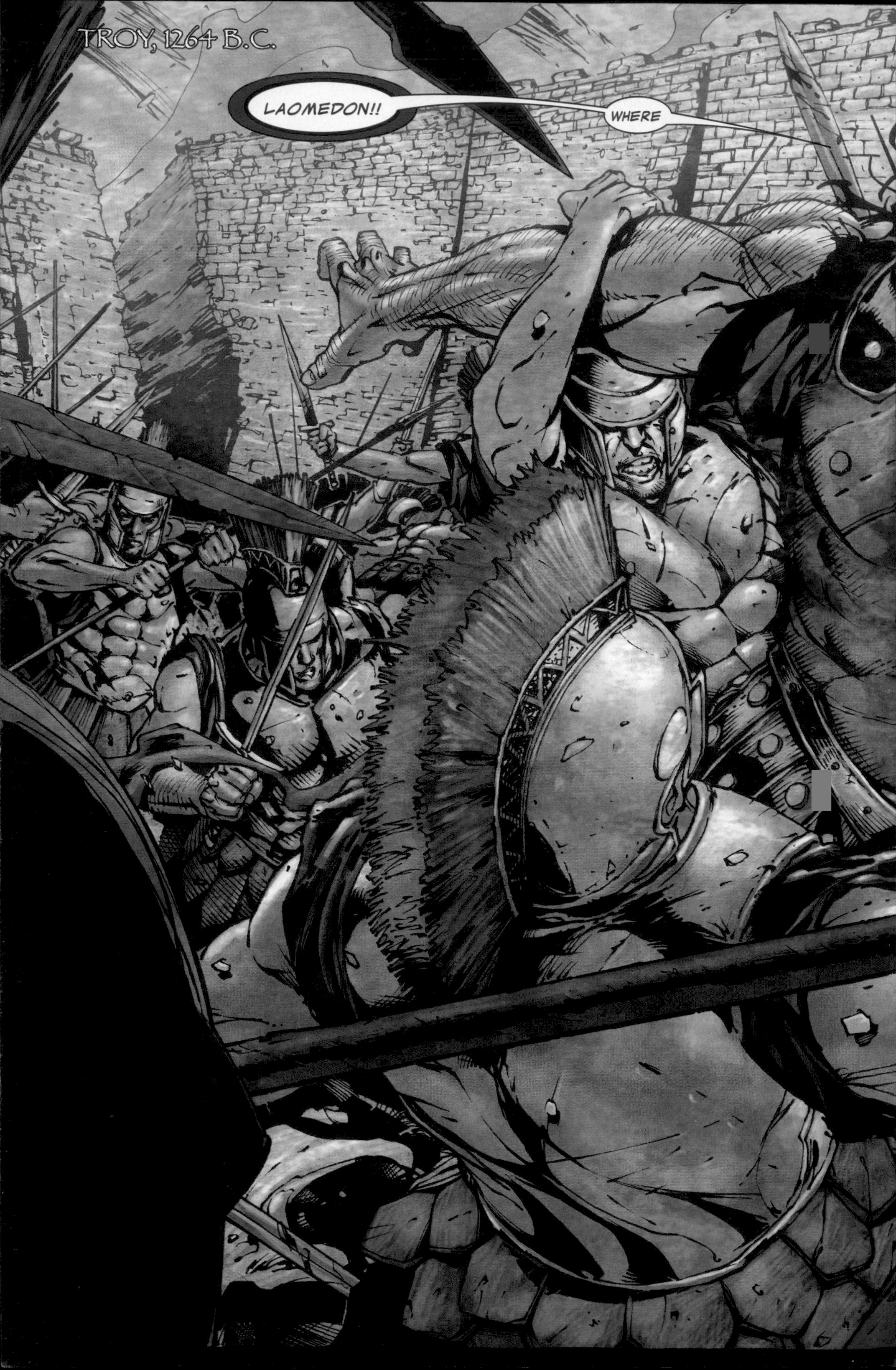
TROY, 1264 B.C.
LAOMEDON!!
WHERE

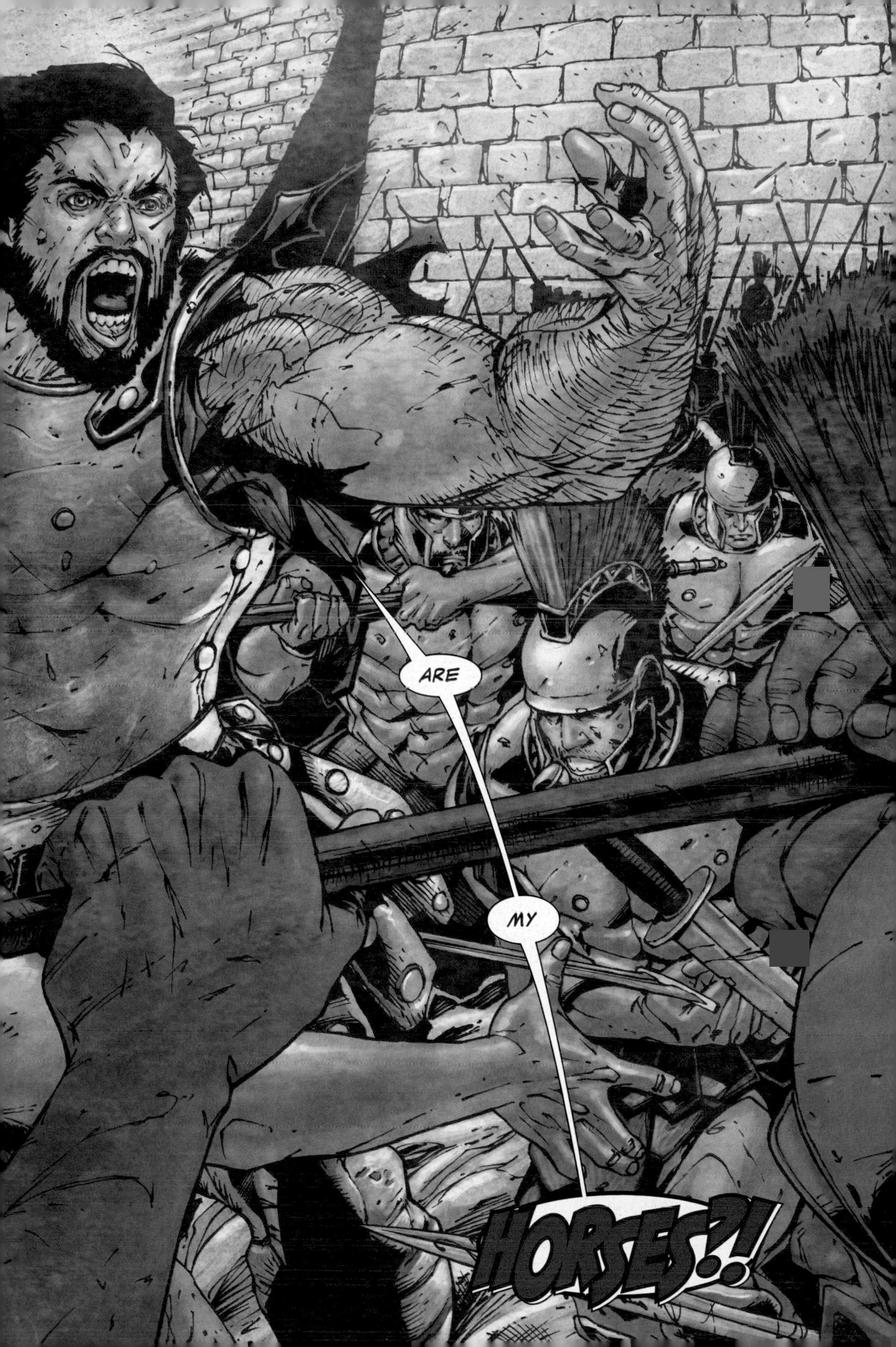
ARE
MY
HORSES?!

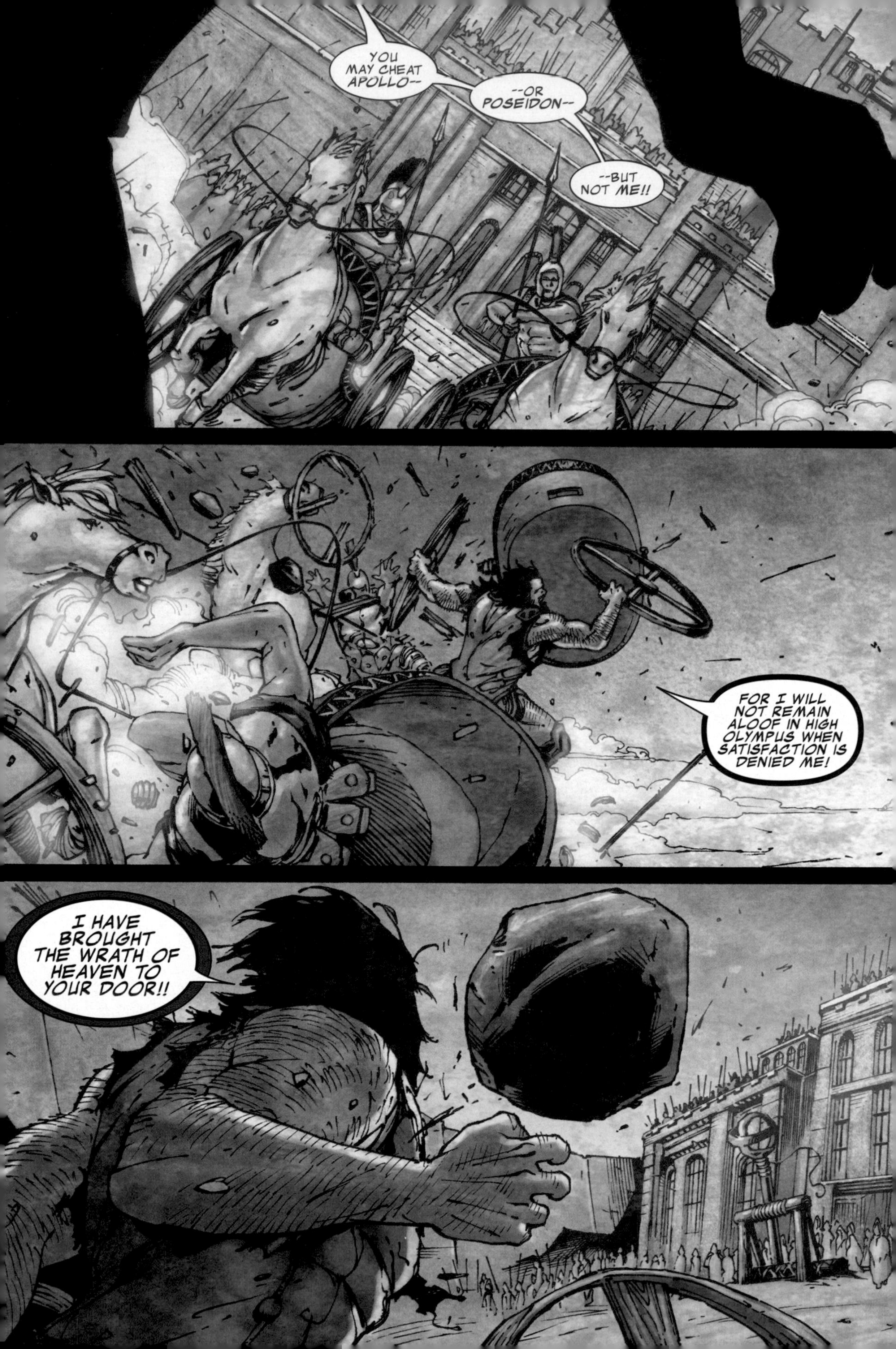
YOU MAY CHEAT APOLLO--
--OR POSEIDON--
--BUT NOT ME!!
FOR I WILL NOT REMAIN ALOOF IN HIGH OLYMPUS WHEN SATISFACTION IS DENIED ME!
I HAVE BROUGHT THE WRATH OF HEAVEN TO YOUR DOOR!!

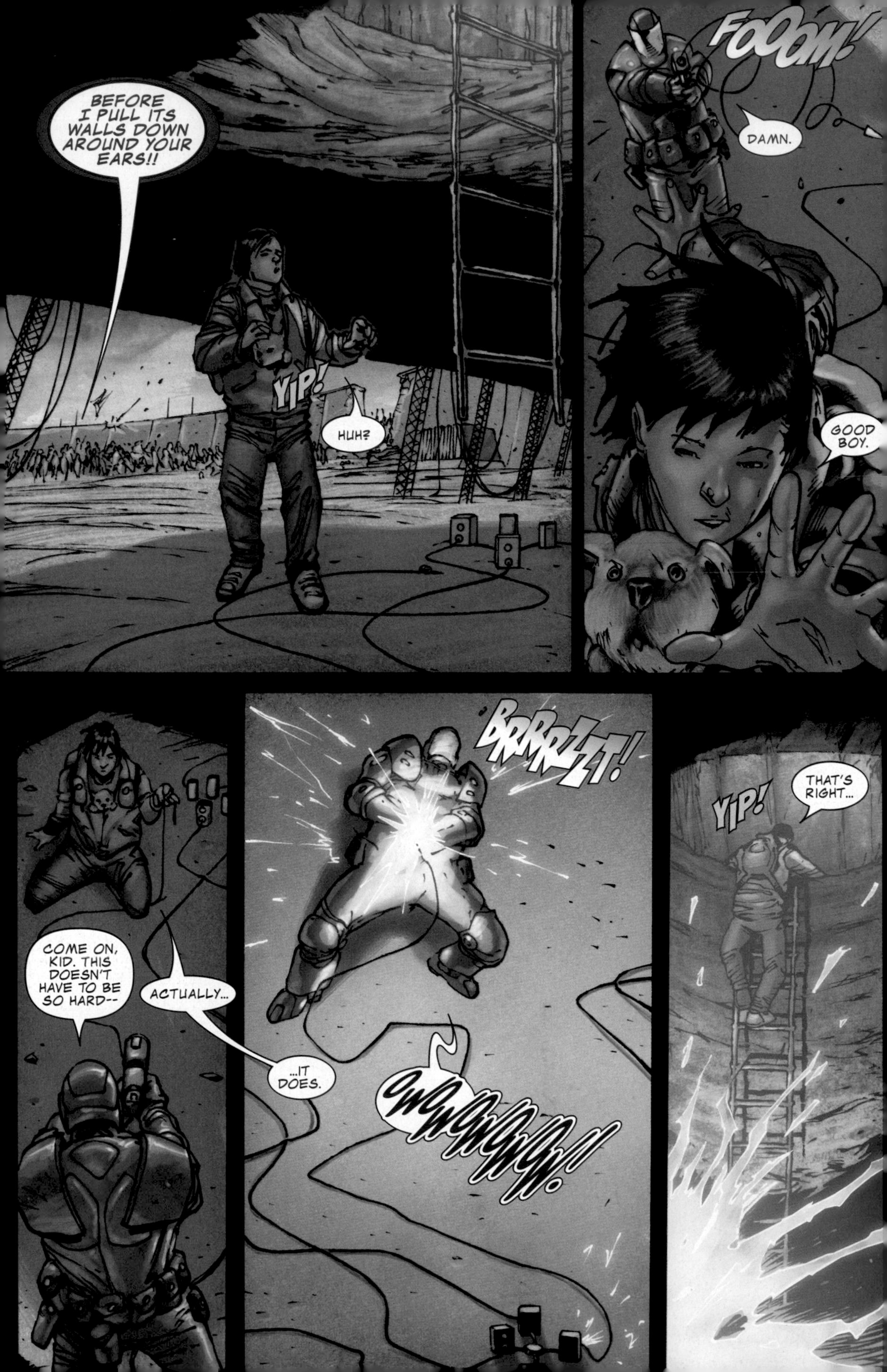
BEFORE I PULL ITS WALLS DOWN AROUND YOUR EARS!!
YIP!
HUH?
FOOOM!
DAMN.
GOOD BOY.
COME ON, KID. THIS DOESN'T HAVE TO BE SO HARD--
ACTUALLY...
...IT DOES.
BRRRZZT!
OWOWOWOW!
YIP!
THAT'S RIGHT...

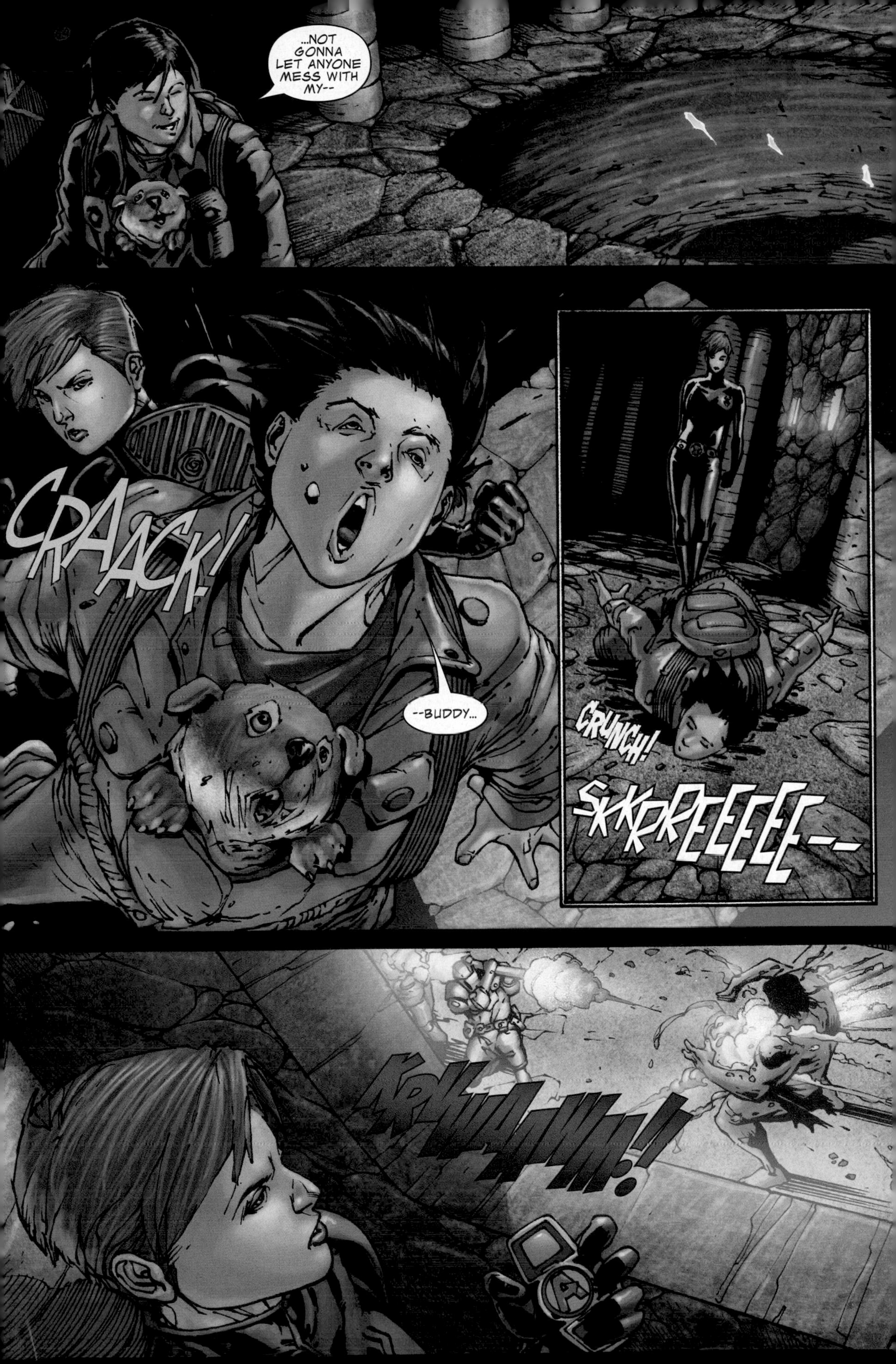
...NOT GONNA LET ANYONE MESS WITH MY--
CRAACK!
--BUDDY...
CRUNCH!
SKKREEEEEE--
KRHHHHHHH!!

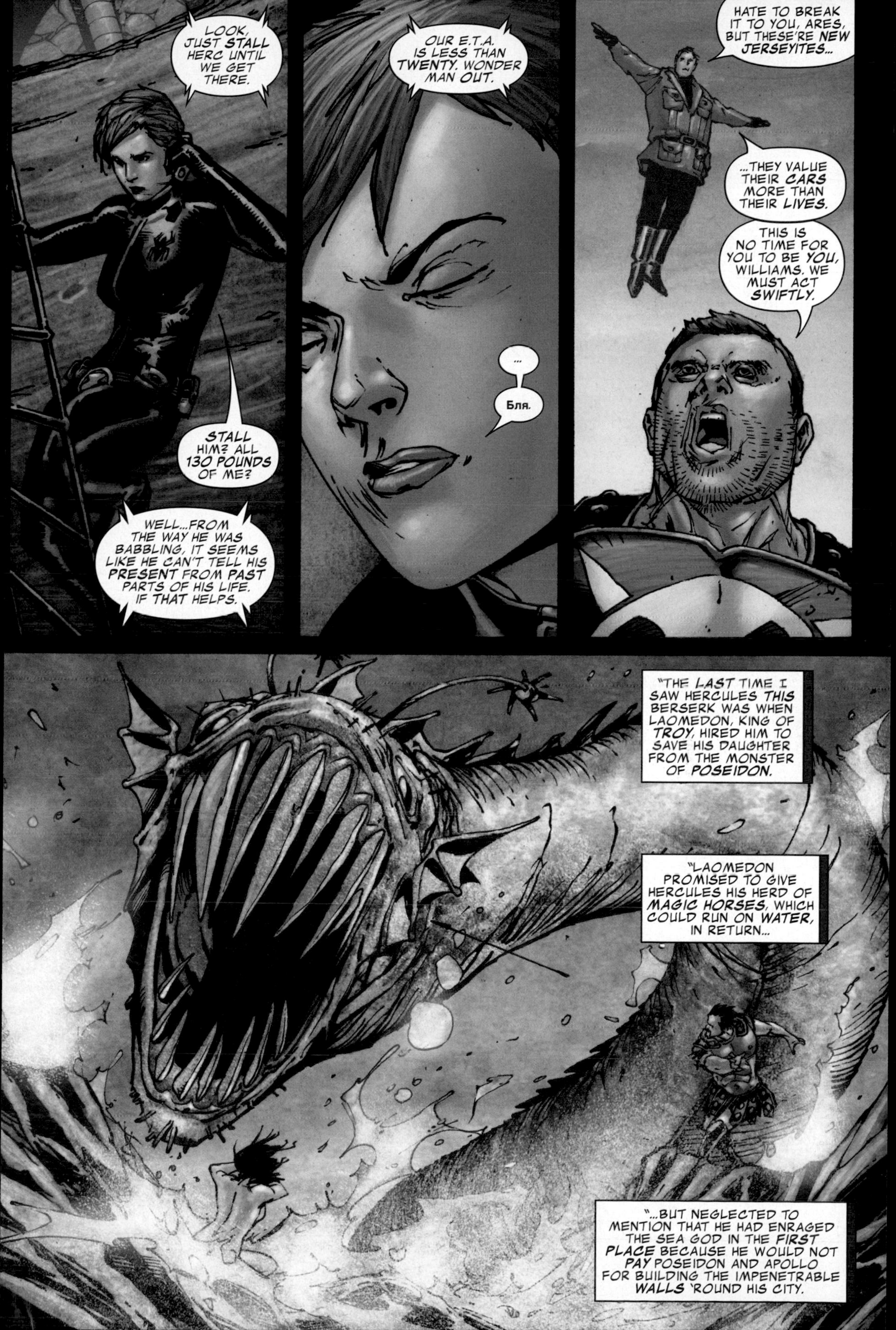
LOOK, JUST STALL HERC UNTIL WE GET THERE.
STALL HIM? ALL 130 POUNDS OF ME?
WELL...FROM THE WAY HE WAS BABBLING, IT SEEMS LIKE HE CAN'T TELL HIS PRESENT FROM PAST PARTS OF HIS LIFE. IF THAT HELPS.
OUR E.T.A. IS LESS THAN TWENTY. WONDER MAN OUT.
...
Бля.
HATE TO BREAK IT TO YOU, ARES, BUT THESE'RE NEW JERSEYITES...
...THEY VALUE THEIR CARS MORE THAN THEIR LIVES.
THIS IS NO TIME FOR YOU TO BE YOU, WILLIAMS. WE MUST ACT SWIFTLY.
"THE LAST TIME I SAW HERCULES THIS BERSERK WAS WHEN LAOMEDON, KING OF TROY, HIRED HIM TO SAVE HIS DAUGHTER FROM THE MONSTER OF POSEIDON.
"LAOMEDON PROMISED TO GIVE HERCULES HIS HERD OF MAGIC HORSES, WHICH COULD RUN ON WATER, IN RETURN...
"...BUT NEGLECTED TO MENTION THAT HE HAD ENRAGED THE SEA GOD IN THE FIRST PLACE BECAUSE HE WOULD NOT PAY POSEIDON AND APOLLO FOR BUILDING THE IMPENETRABLE WALLS 'ROUND HIS CITY.

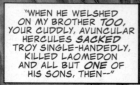

"WHEN HE WELSHED ON MY BROTHER *TOO*, YOUR CUDDLY, AVUNCULAR HERCULES *SACKED* TROY SINGLE-HANDEDLY, KILLED LAOMEDON AND ALL BUT *ONE* OF HIS SONS, THEN--"

YEAH, OKAY, WHATEVER. ENOUGH *EDITH HAMILTON* FOR ONE DAY, HUH?

FOR SOMEBODY WHO SUPPOSEDLY *HATES* HERC SO MUCH, YOU SURE AS HELL CAN'T SEEM TO *SHUT UP* ABOUT HIM...

HEY... WAIT A MINUTE...

THIS IS WHAT YOU WANTED ALL ALONG! YOU *KNEW* THE HYDRA BLOOD WOULD DRIVE HERC NUTSO--

FORCING THE AVENGERS AND WHOEVER ELSE TO USE *MAXIMUM FORCE* TO BRING HIM DOWN!

I DON'T KNOW *WHAT* YOU'RE TALKING ABOUT...

NO WONDER YOU SEEMED SO HOT TO PARTNER WITH *ME* ON THIS DEAL!

YOU THINK I'VE GOT *"CHUMP"* TATTOOED ON MY FOREHEAD, DON'T YOU--

SKREEEEEECH!

OHMIGAWD!!

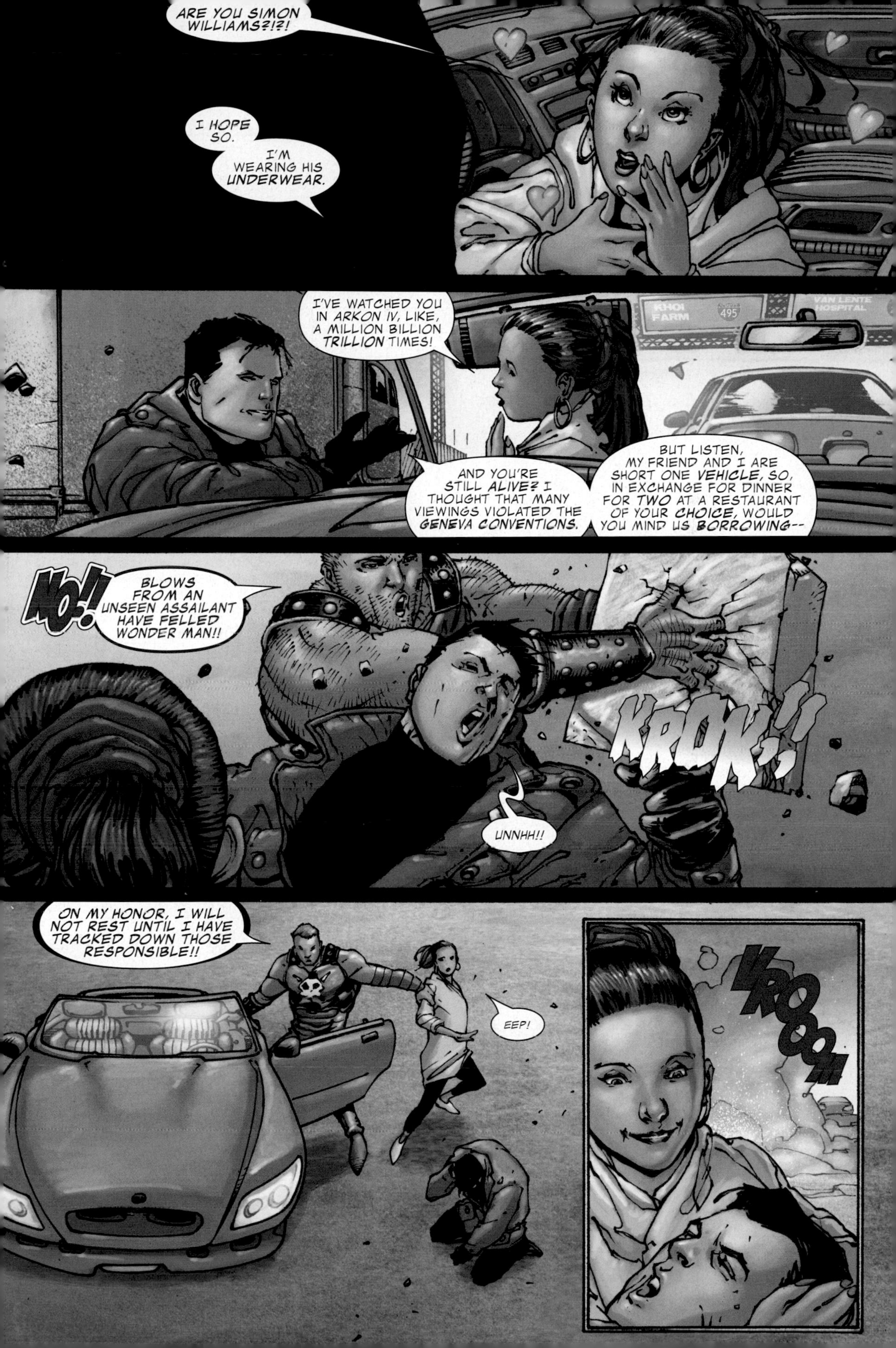
ARE YOU SIMON WILLIAMS?!?!
I HOPE SO.
I'M WEARING HIS UNDERWEAR.
I'VE WATCHED YOU IN ARKON IV, LIKE, A MILLION BILLION TRILLION TIMES!
KHOI FARM
495
VAN LENTE HOSPITAL
AND YOU'RE STILL ALIVE? I THOUGHT THAT MANY VIEWINGS VIOLATED THE GENEVA CONVENTIONS.
BUT LISTEN, MY FRIEND AND I ARE SHORT ONE VEHICLE, SO, IN EXCHANGE FOR DINNER FOR TWO AT A RESTAURANT OF YOUR CHOICE, WOULD YOU MIND US BORROWING--
NO!!
BLOWS FROM AN UNSEEN ASSAILANT HAVE FELLED WONDER MAN!!
KROK!!
UNNHH!!
ON MY HONOR, I WILL NOT REST UNTIL I HAVE TRACKED DOWN THOSE RESPONSIBLE!!
EEP!
VROOOM

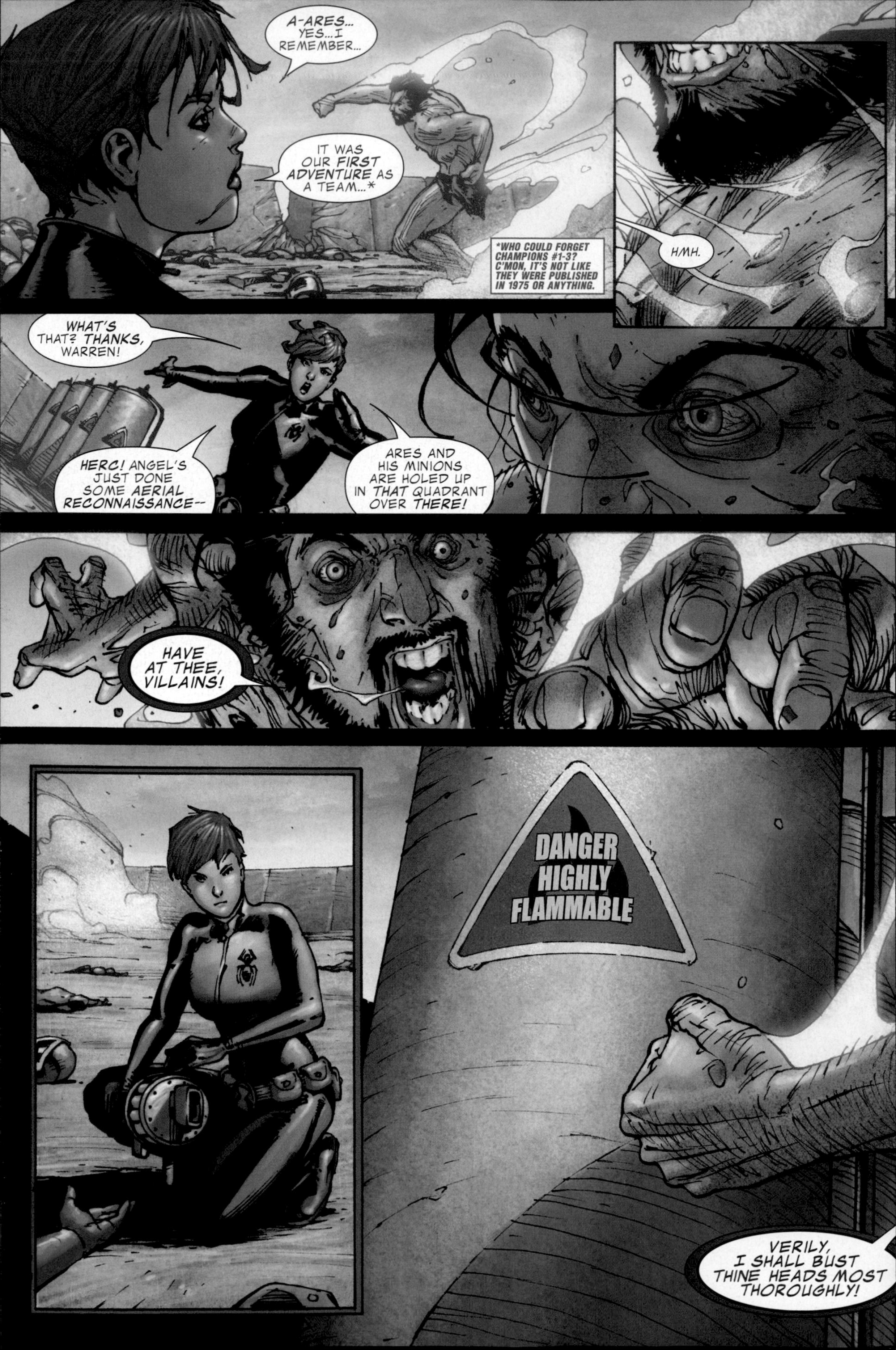
A-ARES... YES...I REMEMBER...
IT WAS OUR FIRST ADVENTURE AS A TEAM...*
*WHO COULD FORGET CHAMPIONS #1-3? C'MON, IT'S NOT LIKE THEY WERE PUBLISHED IN 1975 OR ANYTHING.
HMH.
WHAT'S THAT? THANKS, WARREN!
HERC! ANGEL'S JUST DONE SOME AERIAL RECONNAISSANCE--
ARES AND HIS MINIONS ARE HOLED UP IN THAT QUADRANT OVER THERE!
HAVE AT THEE, VILLAINS!
DANGER HIGHLY FLAMMABLE
VERILY, I SHALL BUST THINE HEADS MOST THOROUGHLY!

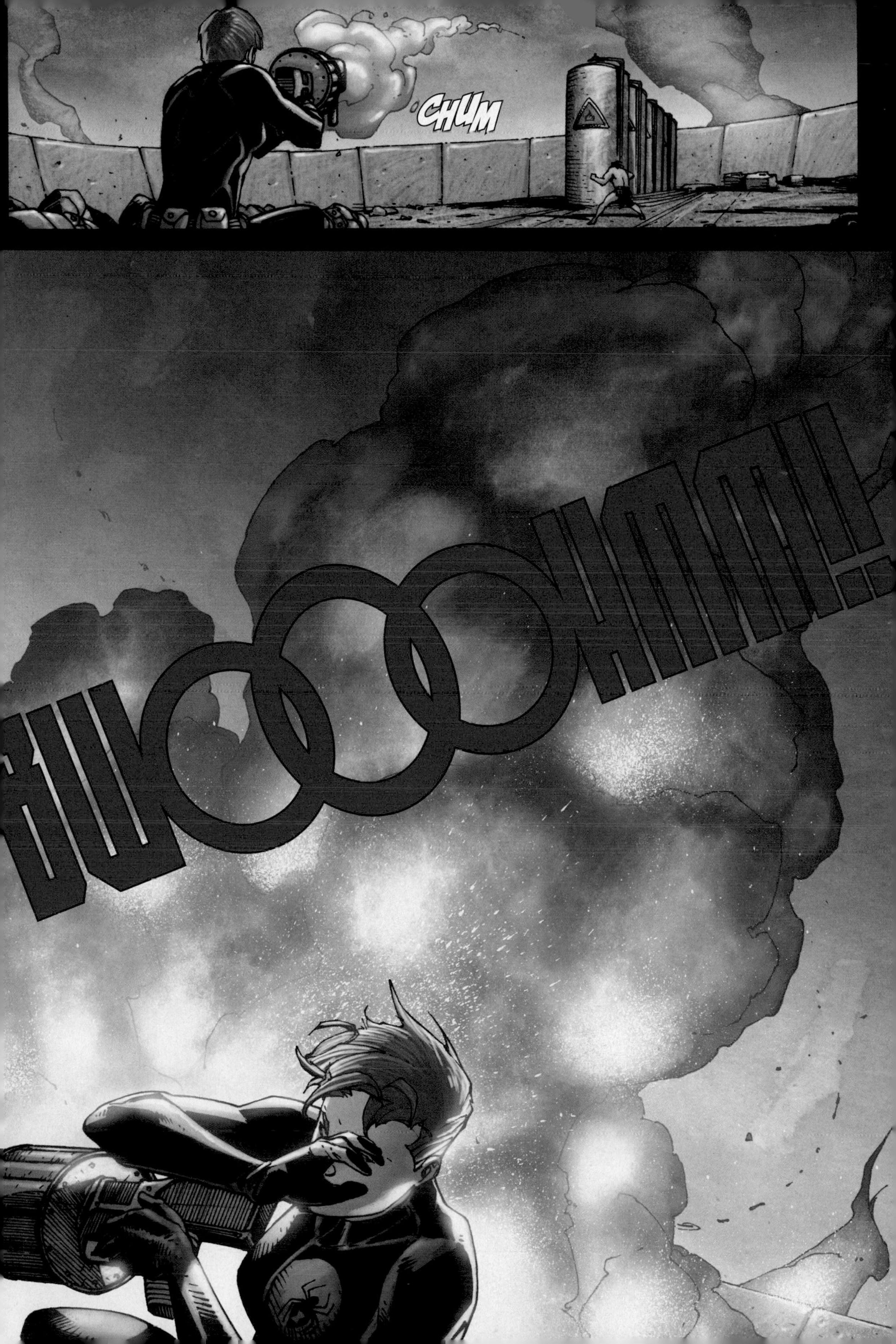
CHUM
BWOOOOMMM!!

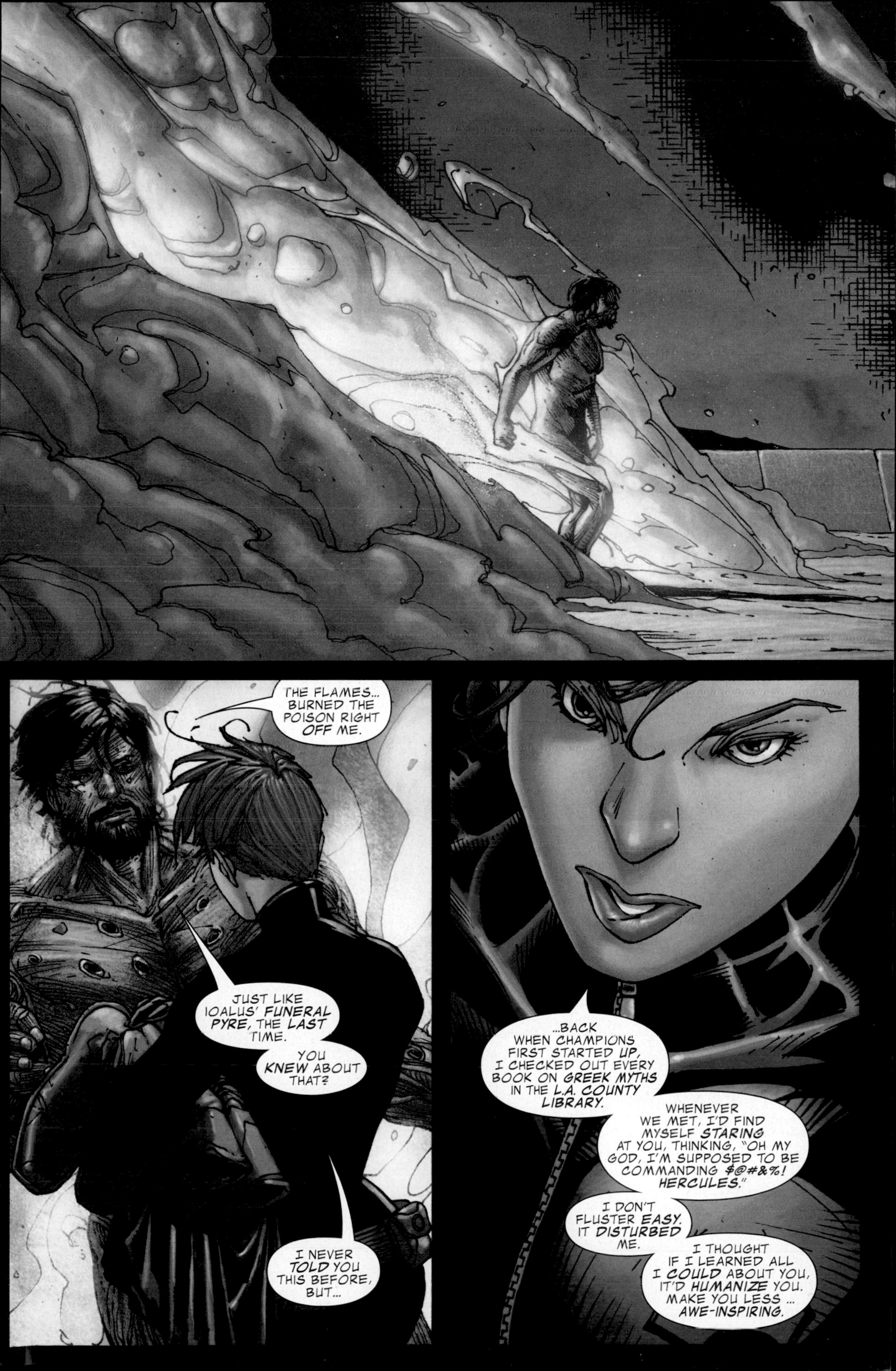

THE FLAMES... BURNED THE POISON RIGHT OFF ME.
JUST LIKE IOALUS' FUNERAL PYRE, THE LAST TIME.
YOU KNEW ABOUT THAT?
I NEVER TOLD YOU THIS BEFORE, BUT...
...BACK WHEN CHAMPIONS FIRST STARTED UP, I CHECKED OUT EVERY BOOK ON GREEK MYTHS IN THE L.A. COUNTY LIBRARY.
WHENEVER WE MET, I'D FIND MYSELF STARING AT YOU, THINKING, "OH MY GOD, I'M SUPPOSED TO BE COMMANDING $@#&%! HERCULES."
I DON'T FLUSTER EASY. IT DISTURBED ME.
I THOUGHT IF I LEARNED ALL I COULD ABOUT YOU, IT'D HUMANIZE YOU. MAKE YOU LESS ... AWE-INSPIRING.

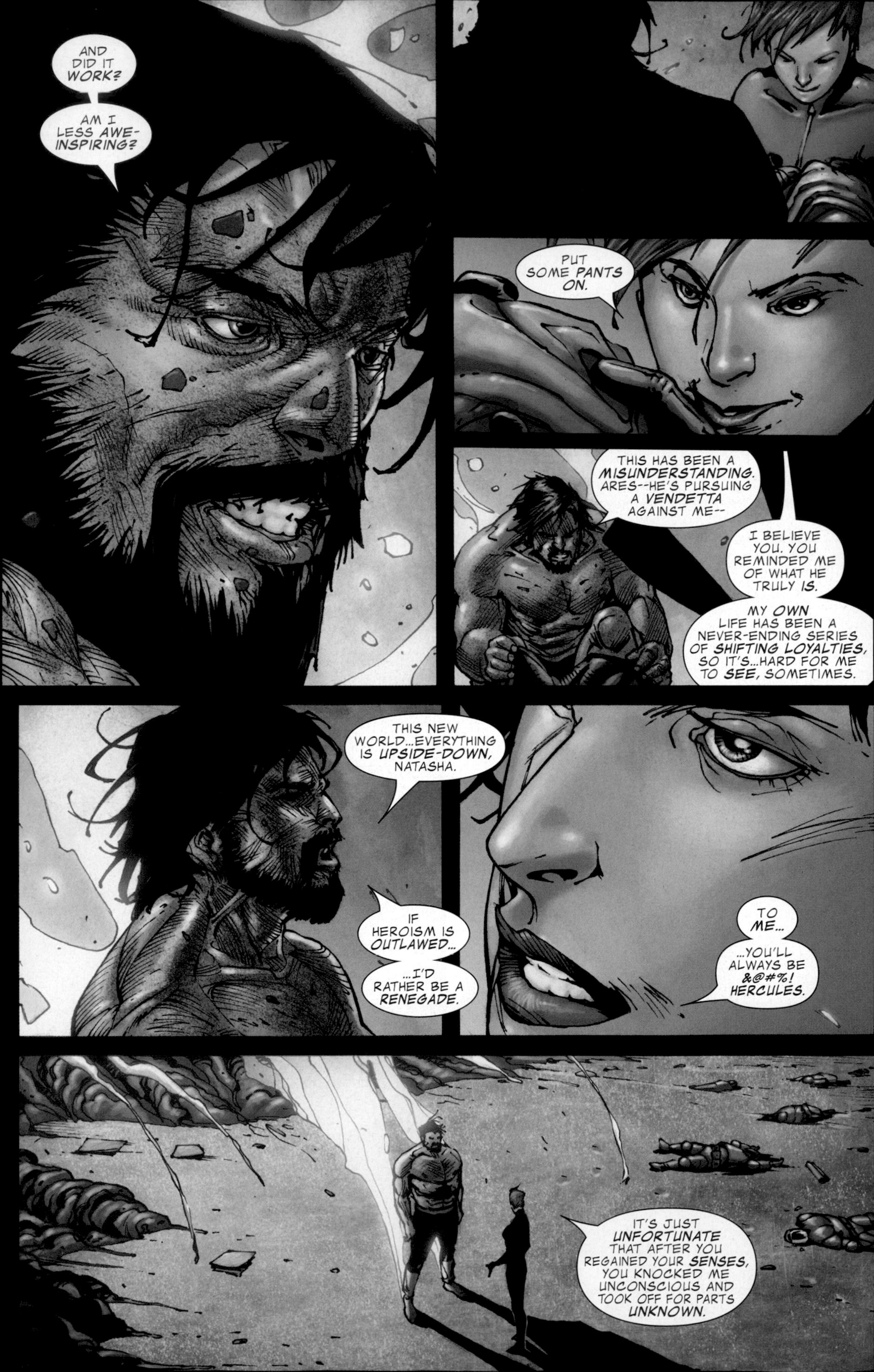
AND DID IT WORK?
AM I LESS AWE-INSPIRING?
PUT SOME PANTS ON.
THIS HAS BEEN A MISUNDERSTANDING. ARES--HE'S PURSUING A VENDETTA AGAINST ME--
I BELIEVE YOU. YOU REMINDED ME OF WHAT HE TRULY IS.
MY OWN LIFE HAS BEEN A NEVER-ENDING SERIES OF SHIFTING LOYALTIES, SO IT'S...HARD FOR ME TO SEE, SOMETIMES.
THIS NEW WORLD...EVERYTHING IS UPSIDE-DOWN, NATASHA.
IF HEROISM IS OUTLAWED...
...I'D RATHER BE A RENEGADE.
TO ME...
...YOU'LL ALWAYS BE &@#%! HERCULES.
IT'S JUST UNFORTUNATE THAT AFTER YOU REGAINED YOUR SENSES, YOU KNOCKED ME UNCONSCIOUS AND TOOK OFF FOR PARTS UNKNOWN.

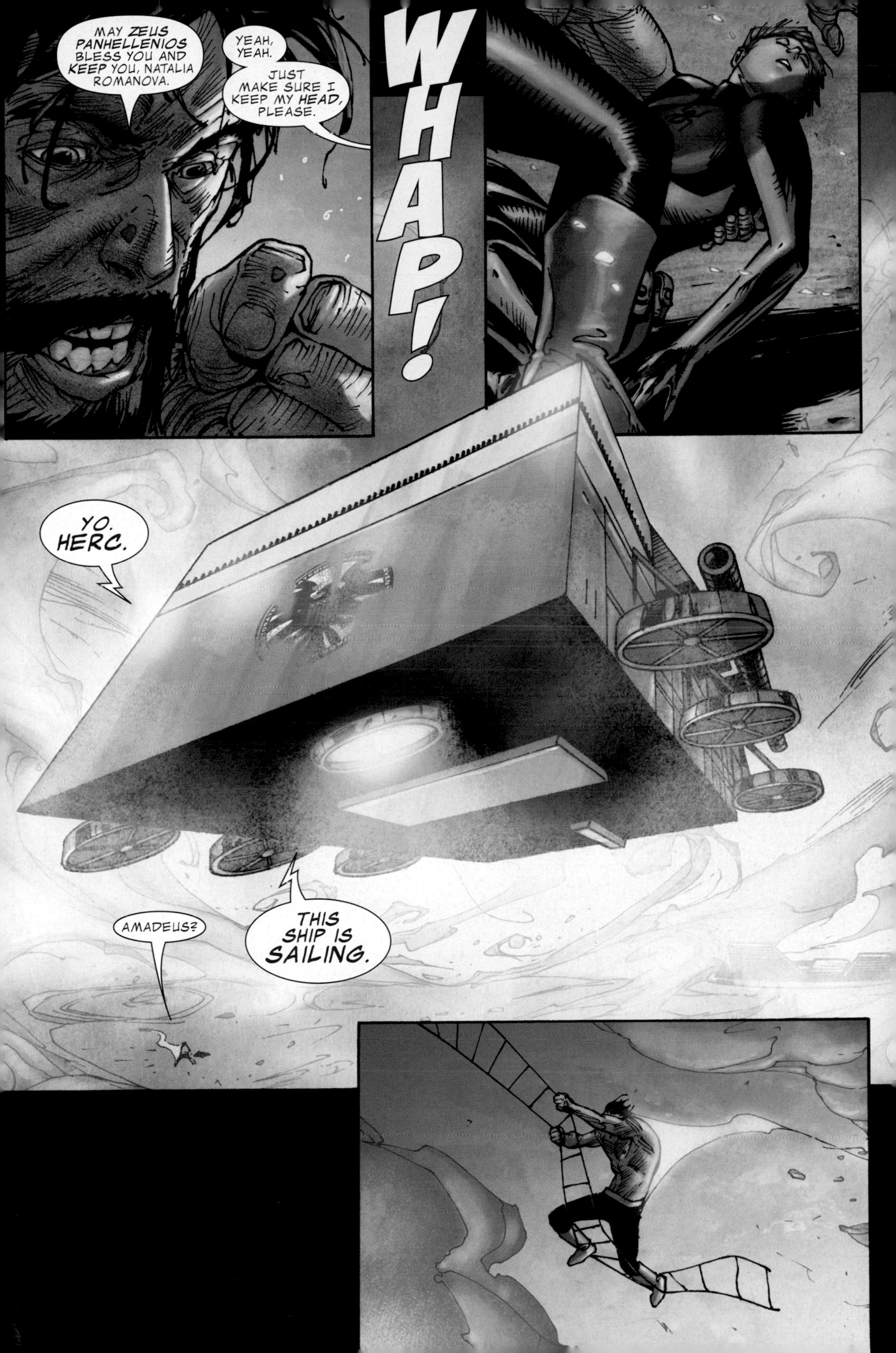
MAY ZEUS PANHELLENIOS BLESS YOU AND KEEP YOU, NATALIA ROMANOVA.
YEAH, YEAH.
JUST MAKE SURE I KEEP MY HEAD, PLEASE.
WHAP!
YO. HERC.
AMADEUS?
THIS SHIP IS SAILING.

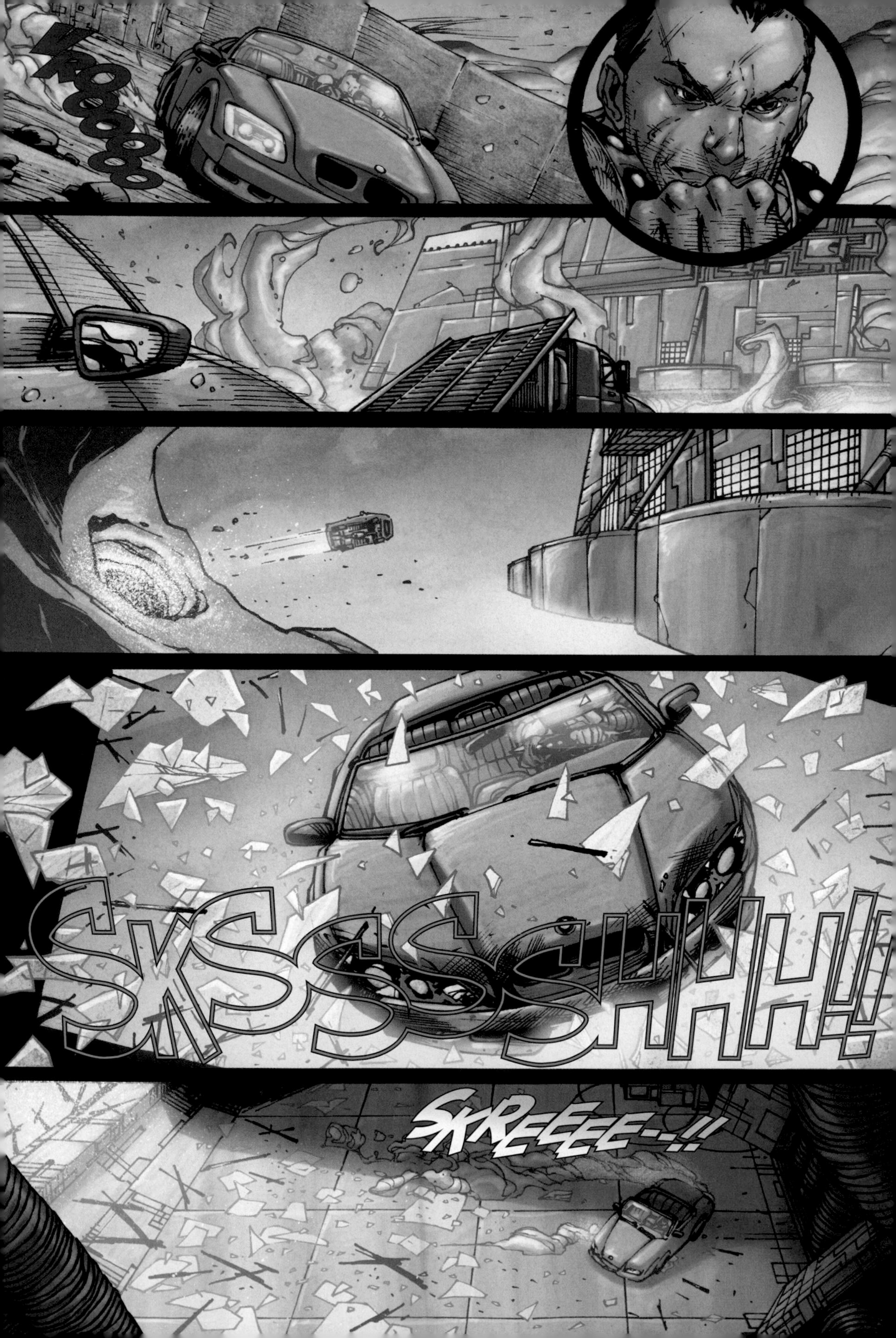
VROOOOOO
SKSSSSCHHHH!!
SKREEEEE--!!

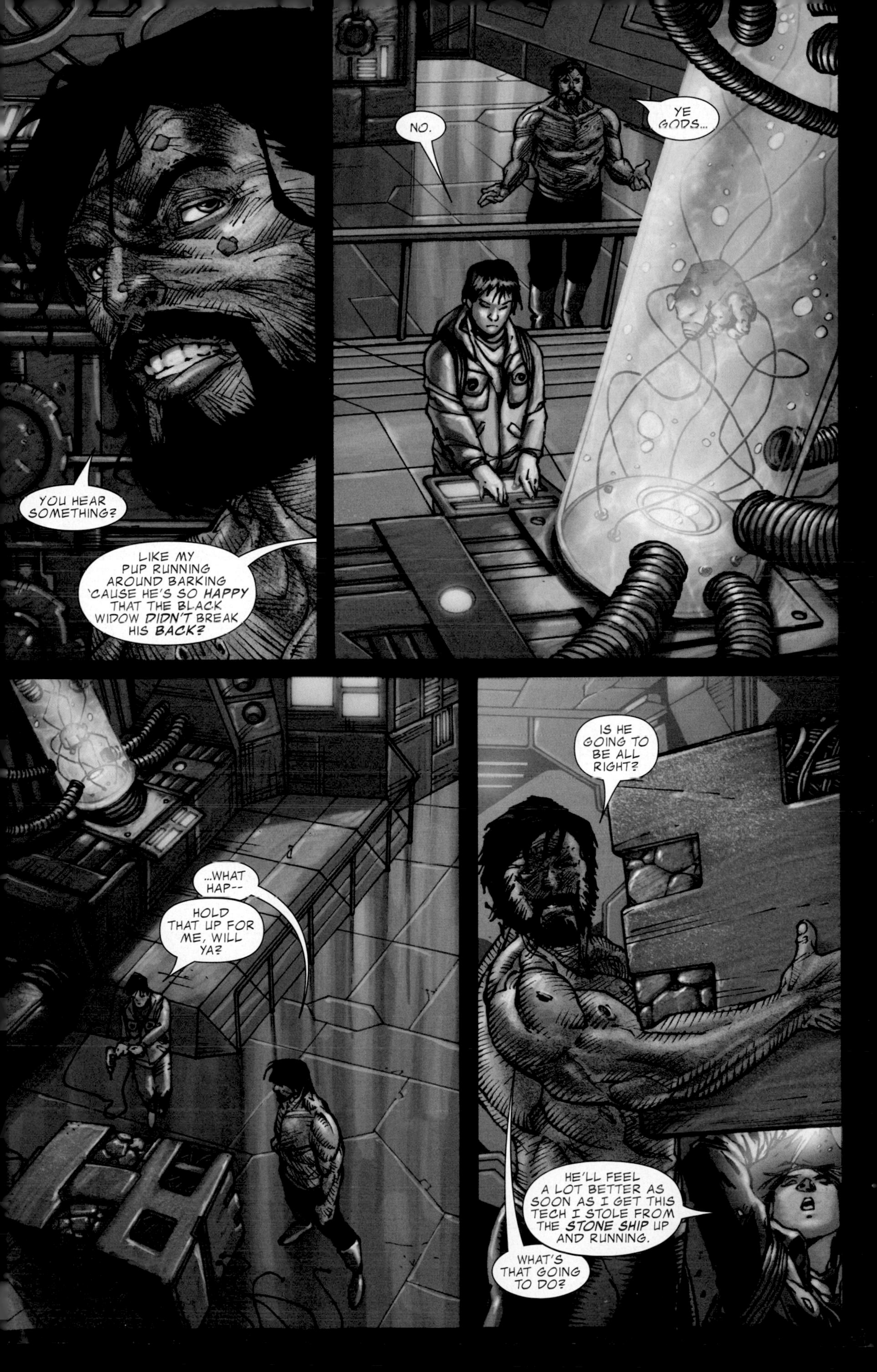
YOU HEAR SOMETHING?
LIKE MY PUP RUNNING AROUND BARKING 'CAUSE HE'S SO HAPPY THAT THE BLACK WIDOW DIDN'T BREAK HIS BACK?
NO.
YE GODS...
...WHAT HAP--
HOLD THAT UP FOR ME, WILL YA?
IS HE GOING TO BE ALL RIGHT?
HE'LL FEEL A LOT BETTER AS SOON AS I GET THIS TECH I STOLE FROM THE STONE SHIP UP AND RUNNING.
WHAT'S THAT GOING TO DO?

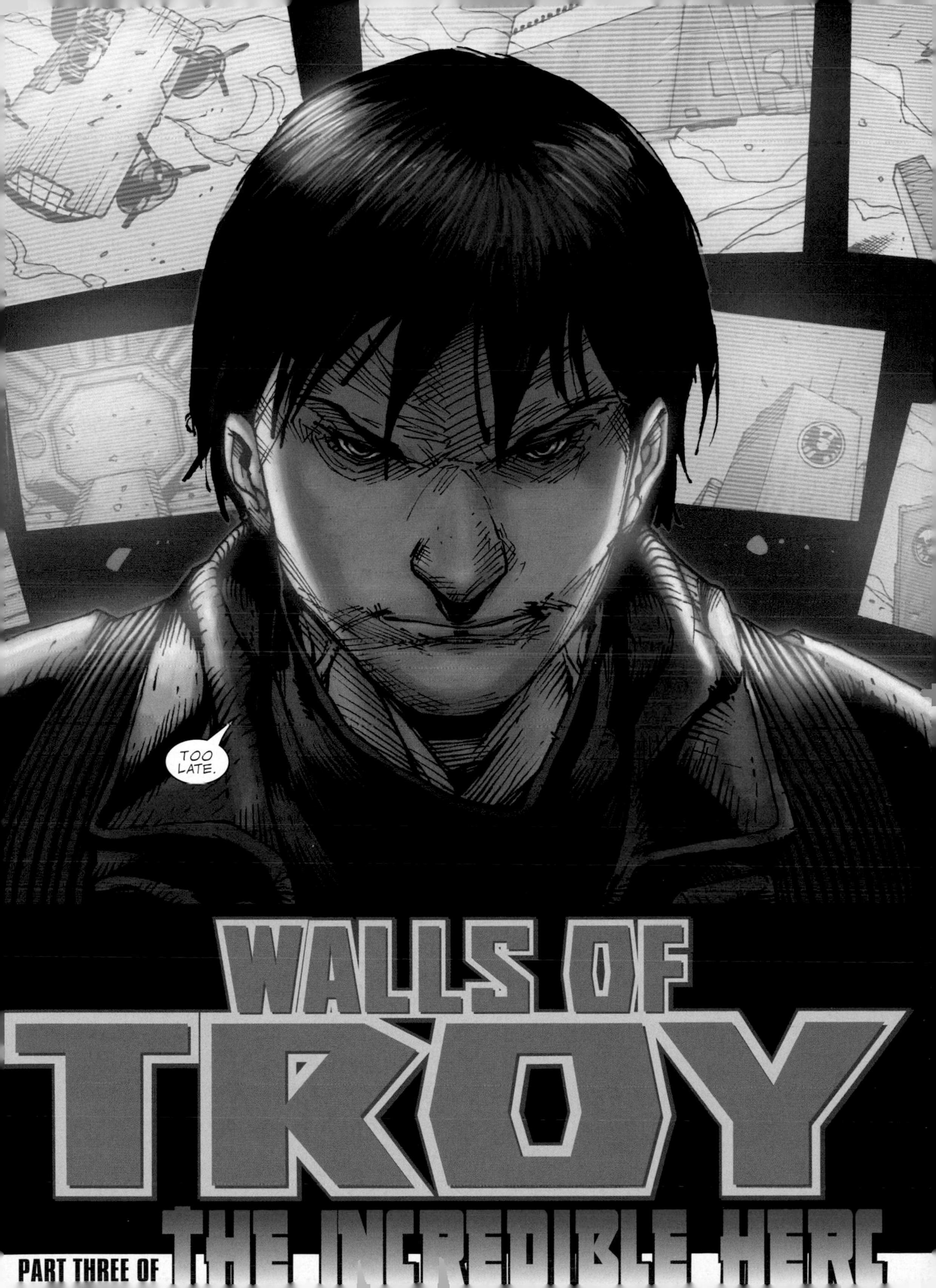
TOO LATE.
WALLS OF TROY
PART THREE OF THE INCREDIBLE HERC

Subject: PUPPY CONTEST
From: THE CHOSTER
Date: 02/13/08
To: ALL

HTTP://WWW.PUPPYCHO.COM

DREAMGRLZ97: he's so cute

HELFRALL0223: name him po! so he can be cho's po!

PANICMP112: CHODESTER!!!!!!!!!

BEEJAIZ1984: cats rule!

POPPYPALS: what about HOWLER!

MANGOGIRL0081: HEY CHO! i think precious would be a puuurfect name! or brighteyes, or snookems, or lady, yeah lady is the best...

KATSEYES113: MY DOG IS BETTER THAN URS!

RICHGHALO7: PLUTOOO!

MUFASSA7272: YAY DAWG! MINES WOULD BEZ SPARKS YO!

MRCOSBIE: YO CHO! NAME HIM KILLA B!

Yo.
This is Cho.

Got a lot on my plate right now.
(as you may have just read)

So while I attempt to take over the world and stuff, I need you name my puppy.

He's a coyote (NOT Wile. E.). His mom's dead (NOT Bambi). He lives inside my jacket (NOT Jake...which is the name of the bird that Brooks keeps in his jacket in Shawshank Redemption. Shut up, I like that movie)

Send your name ideas to:

mondomarvel@marvel.com

You can call this a "contest" if ya want, but it's in no way, shape, or form fair. I'm naming him whatever I want. Might be one of your names, might be something Herc comes up with.

--No mo' Cho

THIS IS THE NAME THE PUPPY CONTEST PAGE WE PUT INTO HERC #114. WE GOT OVER 150 RESPONSES FOR THIS SUCKER (NOTE: THE CONTEST IS OVER, BUT FEEL FREE TO KEEP SENDING IN IDEAS).
--ASSISTANT EDITOR NATHAN COSBY

THE MORE THOU KNOWEST

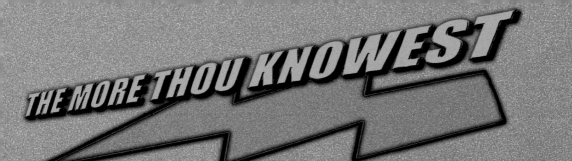

THINKEST THOU LIFE IS ALL MUTTON AND MAIDENS?

NAY.

CONSIDER POWERFUL **HERCULES.** GREATEST OF HEROES. PARAGON OF MASCULINITY. HIS SHOULD BE A LIFE OF GRANDEUR.

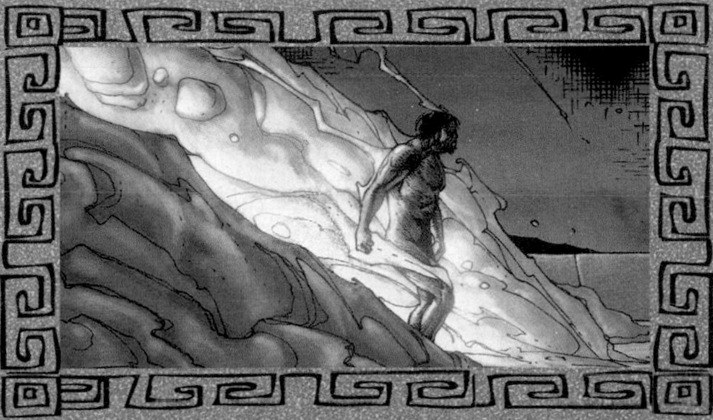

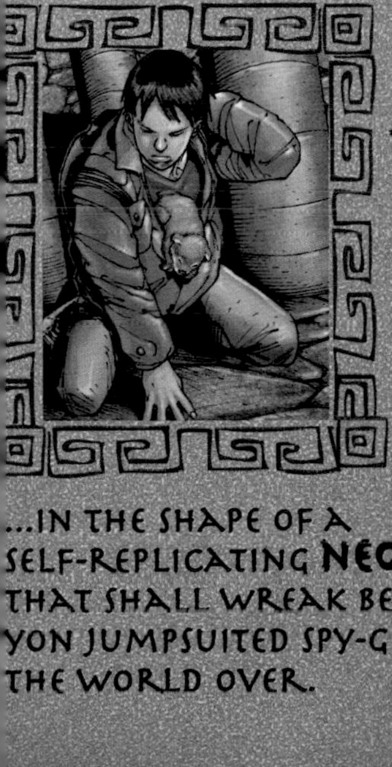

AND YET THE PATHWAY HERCULES TREADS IS FRAUGHT WITH PERIL, THROUGH FAULT PRINCIPALLY OF **AMADEUS CHO** (WITH PUP IN TOW).

CHO DEEMS S.H.I.E.L.D. RESPONSIBLE FOR WOUNDING HIS PUP, AND SO A FURIOUS CAN OF GANGSTA-STYLE WHUP-@$$ DESCENDS UPON THE MORTAL ENFORCEMENT AGENCY...

...IN THE SHAPE OF A SELF-REPLICATING **NEO-VIRUS** THAT SHALL WREAK BEDLAM UPON YON JUMPSUITED SPY-GUYS' OPERATIONS THE WORLD OVER.

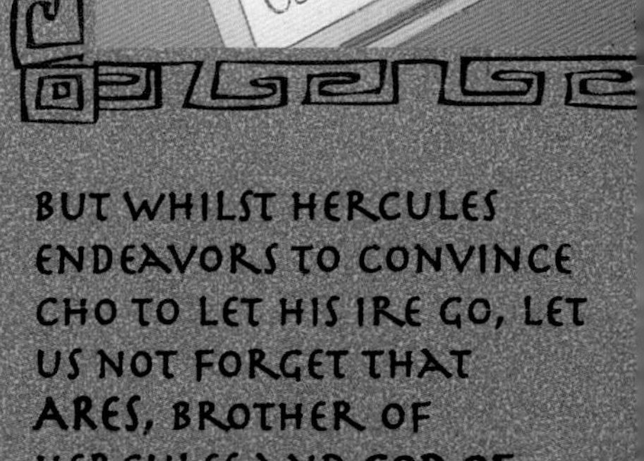
OS Chowned 1.0

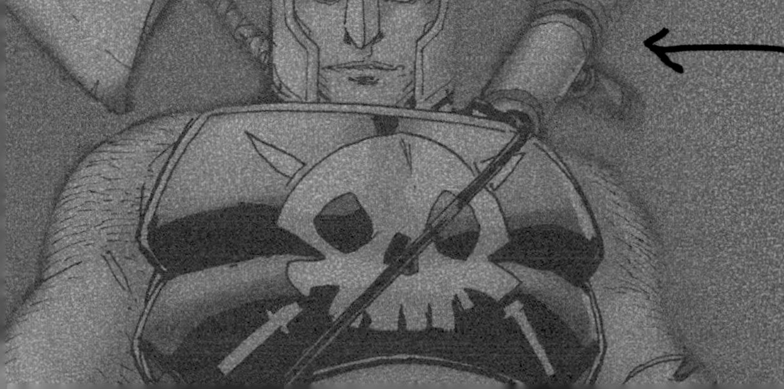

BUT WHILST HERCULES ENDEAVORS TO CONVINCE CHO TO LET HIS IRE GO, LET US NOT FORGET THAT **ARES**, BROTHER OF HERCULES AND GOD OF #%*&IN' WAR, WAITS TO STRIKE...

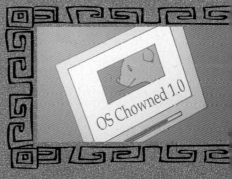

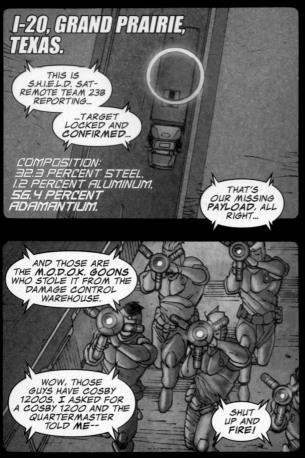

I-20, GRAND PRAIRIE, TEXAS.

THIS IS S.H.I.E.L.D. SAT-REMOTE TEAM 23B REPORTING...

...TARGET LOCKED AND CONFIRMED...

COMPOSITION: 32.3 PERCENT STEEL, 1.2 PERCENT ALUMINUM, 56.4 PERCENT ADAMANTIUM.

THAT'S OUR MISSING PAYLOAD, ALL RIGHT...

AND THOSE ARE THE M.O.D.O.K. GOONS WHO STOLE IT FROM THE DAMAGE CONTROL WAREHOUSE.

WOW, THOSE GUYS HAVE COSBY 1200S. I ASKED FOR A COSBY 1200 AND THE QUARTERMASTER TOLD ME--

SHUT UP AND FIRE!

SHKOOOOOM

THE NEGATIVE ZONE PRISON.

I'M SORRY I DON'T HAVE BETTER NEWS. I HAD TO THREATEN A FEDERAL LAWSUIT JUST TO GET THIS MEETING.

WE UNDERSTAND. WE FOUGHT FOR THE HULK. AND THE HULK WAS YOUR ENEMY. JUST TELL US...

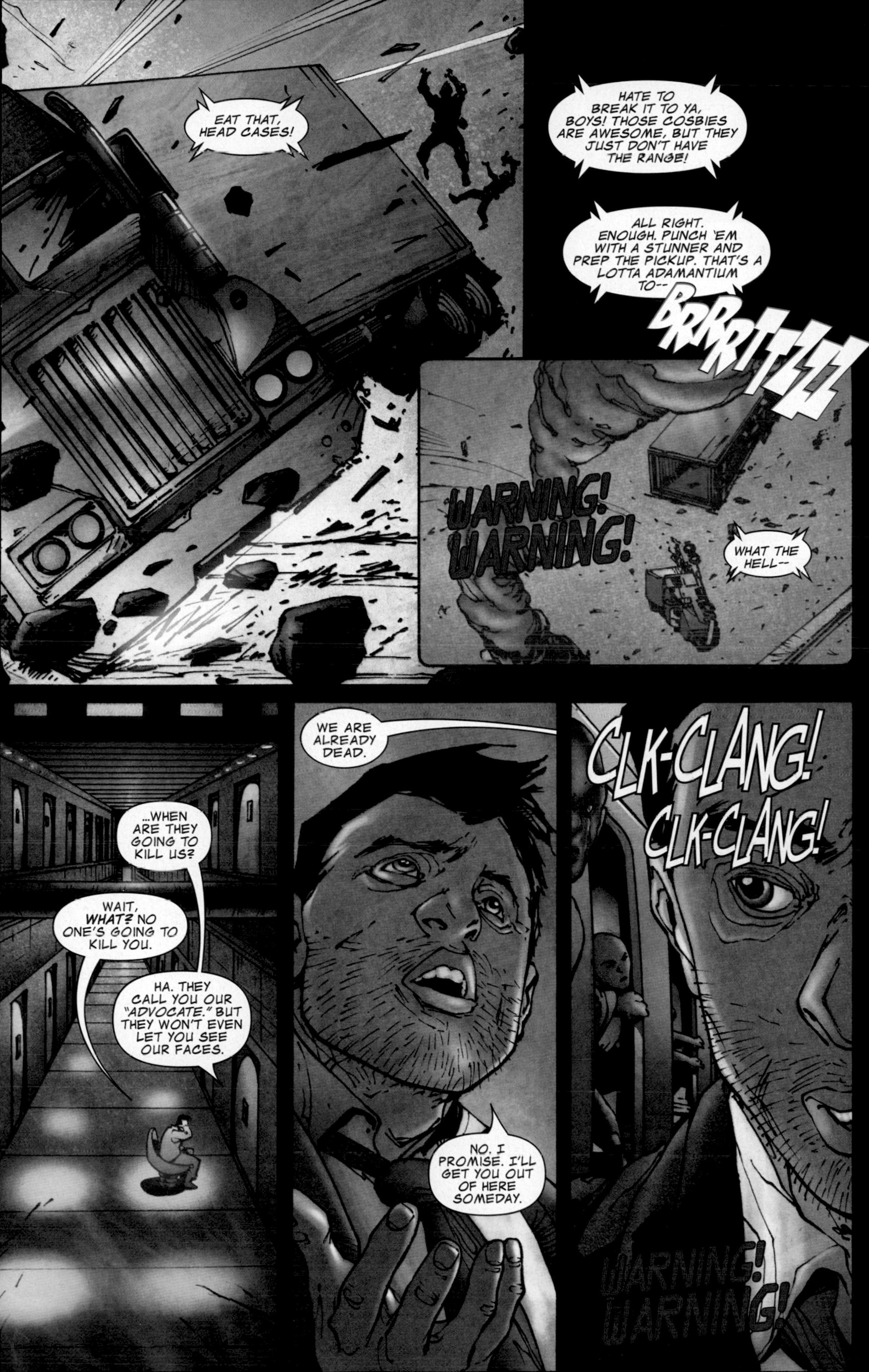
EAT THAT, HEAD CASES!
HATE TO BREAK IT TO YA, BOYS! THOSE COSBIES ARE AWESOME, BUT THEY JUST DON'T HAVE THE RANGE!
ALL RIGHT. ENOUGH. PUNCH 'EM WITH A STUNNER AND PREP THE PICKUP. THAT'S A LOTTA ADAMANTIUM TO--
BRRRRITZZZ
WARNING! WARNING!
WHAT THE HELL--
...WHEN ARE THEY GOING TO KILL US?
WAIT, WHAT? NO ONE'S GOING TO KILL YOU.
HA. THEY CALL YOU OUR "ADVOCATE." BUT THEY WON'T EVEN LET YOU SEE OUR FACES.
WE ARE ALREADY DEAD.
NO. I PROMISE. I'LL GET YOU OUT OF HERE SOMEDAY.
CLK-CLANG! CLK-CLANG!
WARNING! WARNING!

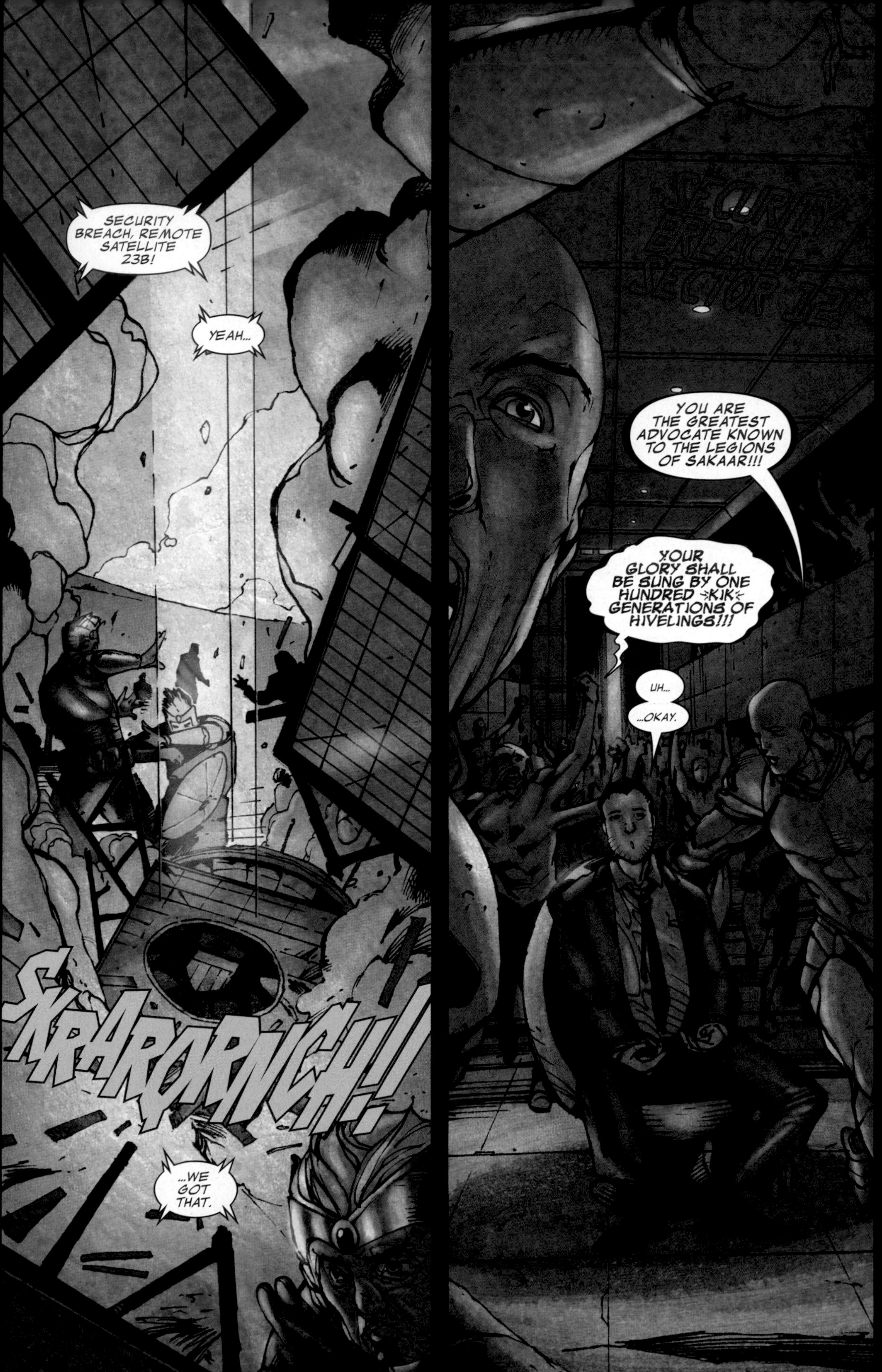
SECURITY BREACH, REMOTE SATELLITE 23B!
YEAH...
SKRARQRNCH!!
...WE GOT THAT.
YOU ARE THE GREATEST ADVOCATE KNOWN TO THE LEGIONS OF SAKAAR!!!
YOUR GLORY SHALL BE SUNG BY ONE HUNDRED ⊰KIK⊱ GENERATIONS OF HIVELINGS!!!
UH...
...OKAY.

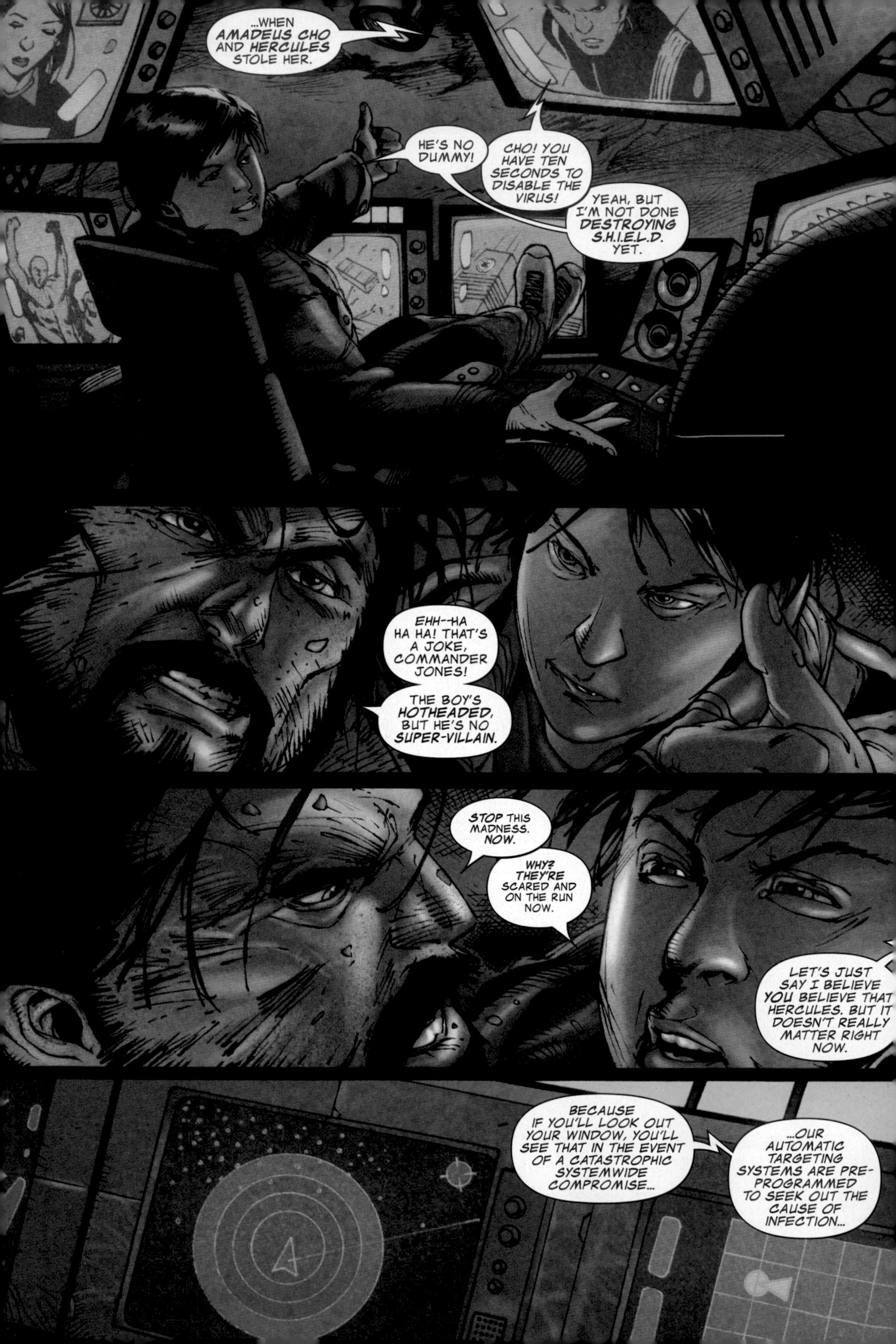
...WHEN AMADEUS CHO AND HERCULES STOLE HER.
HE'S NO DUMMY!
CHO! YOU HAVE TEN SECONDS TO DISABLE THE VIRUS!
YEAH, BUT I'M NOT DONE DESTROYING S.H.I.E.L.D. YET.
EHH--HA HA HA! THAT'S A JOKE, COMMANDER JONES!
THE BOY'S HOTHEADED, BUT HE'S NO SUPER-VILLAIN.
STOP THIS MADNESS. NOW.
WHY? THEY'RE SCARED AND ON THE RUN NOW.
LET'S JUST SAY I BELIEVE YOU BELIEVE THAT HERCULES. BUT IT DOESN'T REALLY MATTER RIGHT NOW.
BECAUSE IF YOU'LL LOOK OUT YOUR WINDOW, YOU'LL SEE THAT IN THE EVENT OF A CATASTROPHIC SYSTEMWIDE COMPROMISE...
...OUR AUTOMATIC TARGETING SYSTEMS ARE PRE-PROGRAMMED TO SEEK OUT THE CAUSE OF INFECTION...

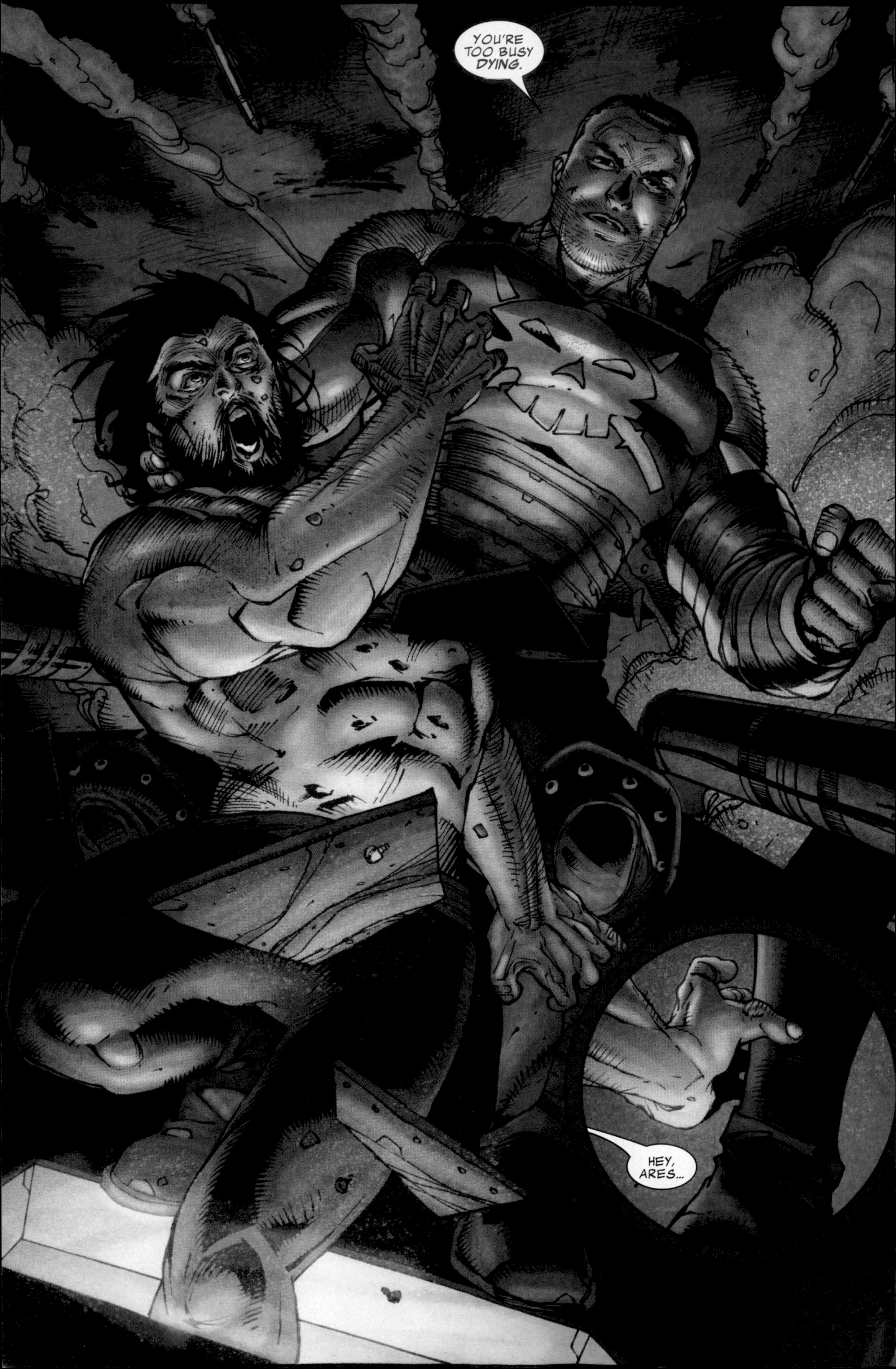
YOU'RE TOO BUSY DYING.
HEY, ARES...

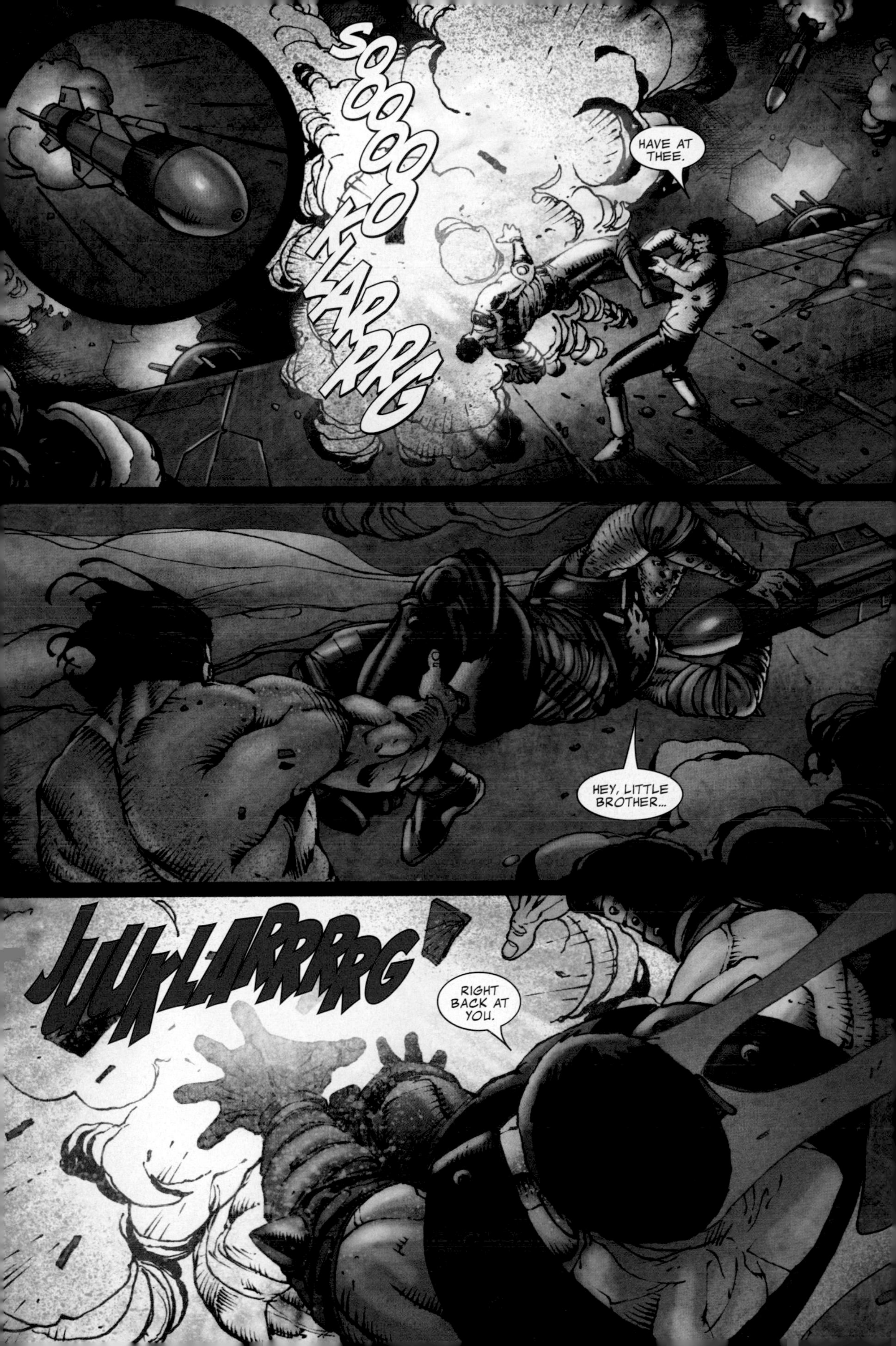

SOOOOOOKLARRRG
HAVE AT THEE.
HEY, LITTLE BROTHER...
JUUKLARRRRG
RIGHT BACK AT YOU.

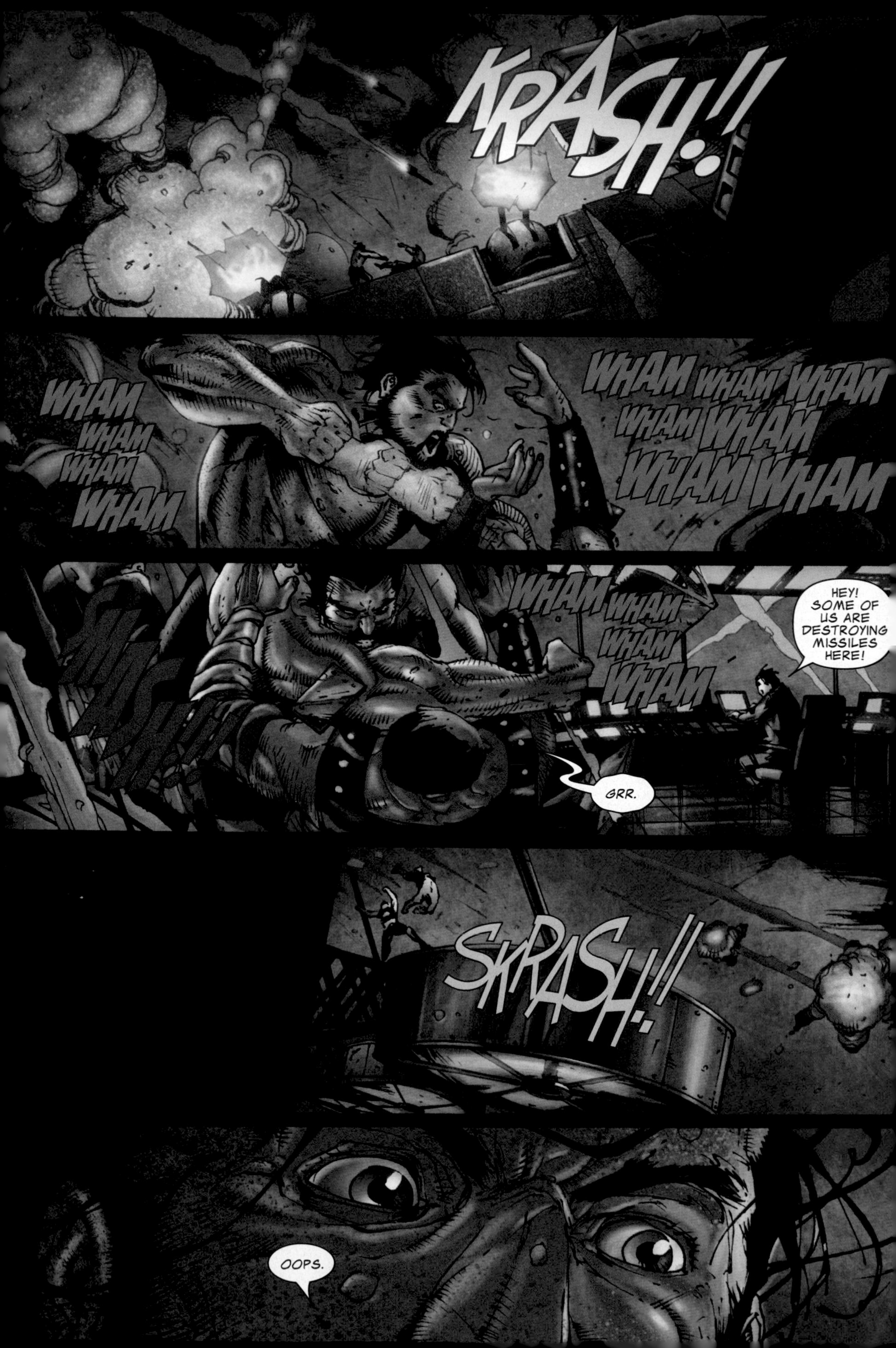
KRASH!!
WHAM
WHAM
WHAM
WHAM
WHAM WHAM WHAM
WHAM WHAM
WHAM WHAM
WHAM
WHAM
WHAM
WHAM
HEY! SOME OF US ARE DESTROYING MISSILES HERE!
GRR.
SKRASH!!
OOPS.

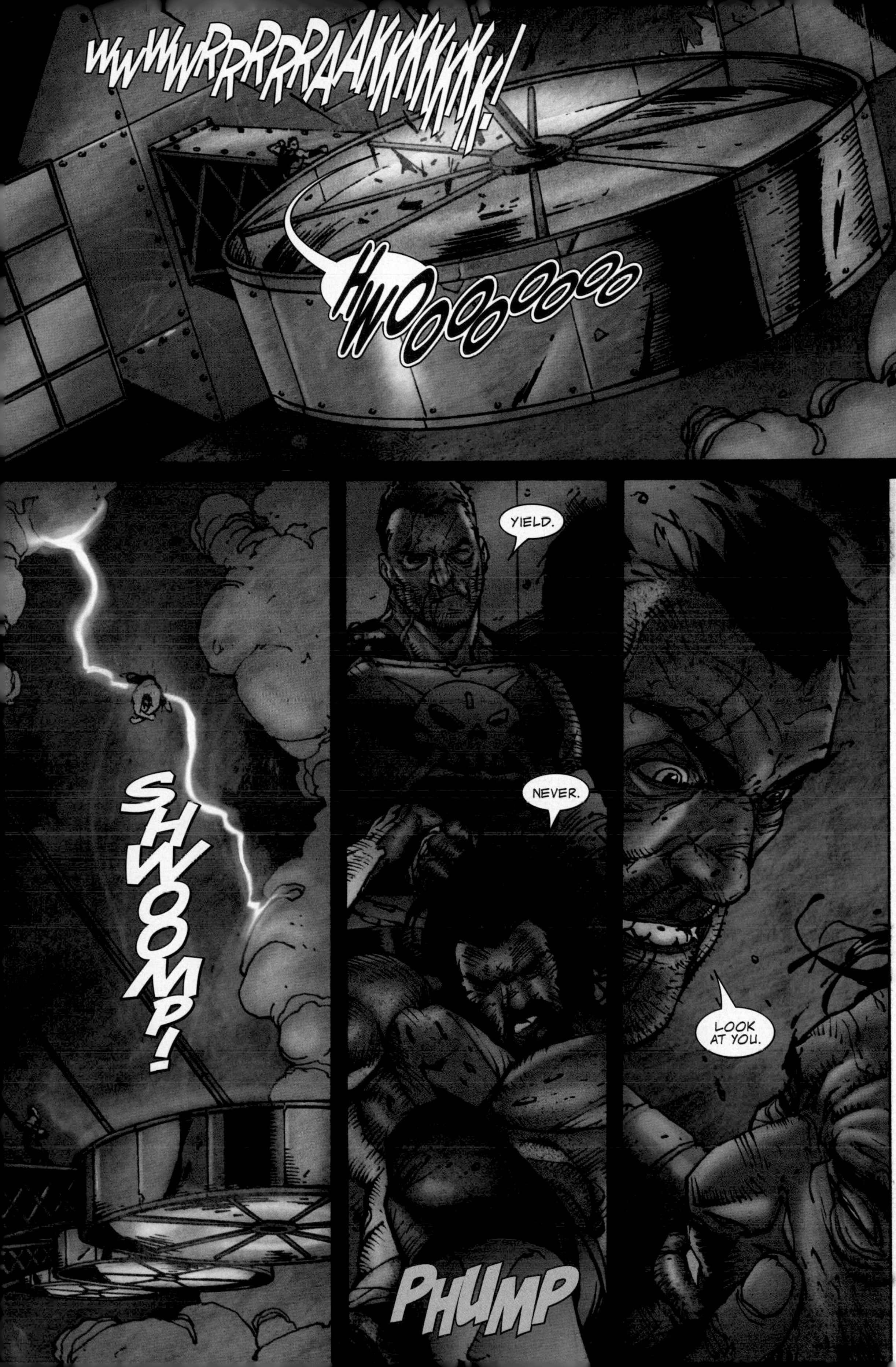
WWWWRRRRRAAKKKKKK!
HWOOOOOOOOO
SHWOOMP!
YIELD.
NEVER.
PHUMP
LOOK AT YOU.

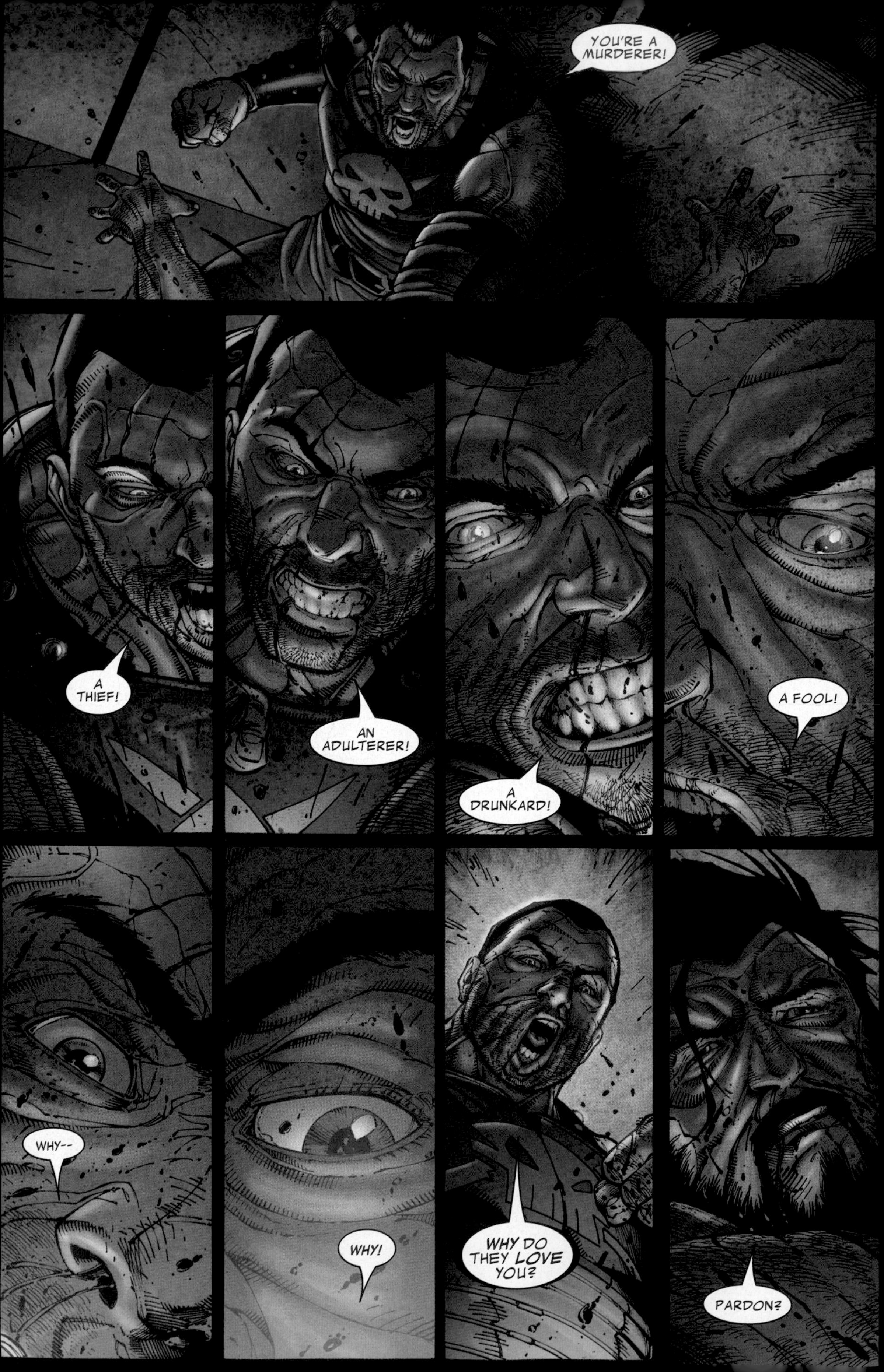
YOU'RE A MURDERER!
A THIEF!
AN ADULTERER!
A DRUNKARD!
A FOOL!
WHY--
WHY!
WHY DO THEY LOVE YOU?
PARDON?

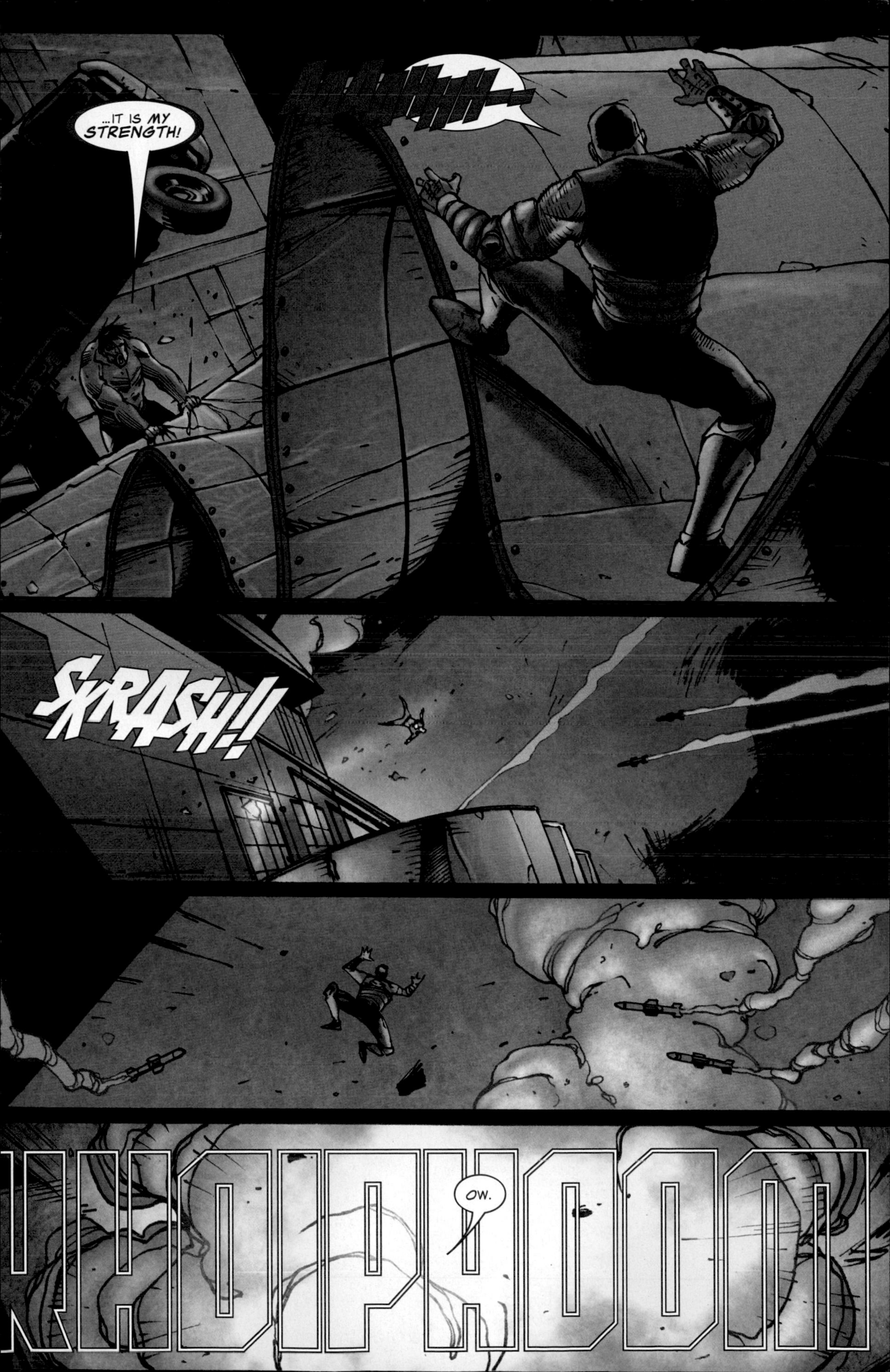
...IT IS MY STRENGTH!
SKRASH!!
KHOIPHOOM
OW.

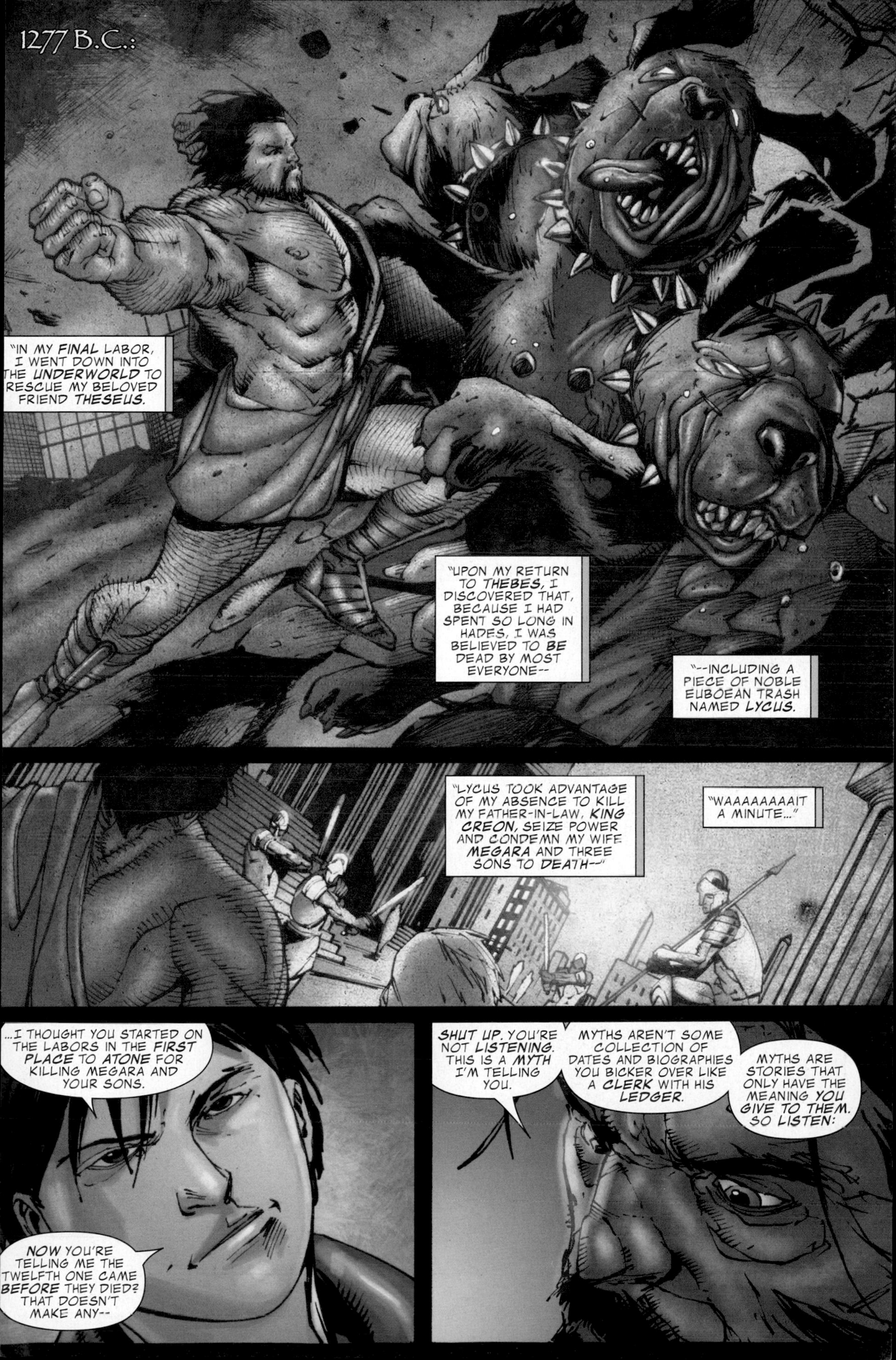
1277 B.C.:
"IN MY FINAL LABOR, I WENT DOWN INTO THE UNDERWORLD TO RESCUE MY BELOVED FRIEND THESEUS.
"UPON MY RETURN TO THEBES, I DISCOVERED THAT, BECAUSE I HAD SPENT SO LONG IN HADES, I WAS BELIEVED TO BE DEAD BY MOST EVERYONE--
"--INCLUDING A PIECE OF NOBLE EUBOEAN TRASH NAMED LYCUS.
"LYCUS TOOK ADVANTAGE OF MY ABSENCE TO KILL MY FATHER-IN-LAW, KING CREON, SEIZE POWER AND CONDEMN MY WIFE MEGARA AND THREE SONS TO DEATH--"
"WAAAAAAAAIT A MINUTE..."
...I THOUGHT YOU STARTED ON THE LABORS IN THE FIRST PLACE TO ATONE FOR KILLING MEGARA AND YOUR SONS.
NOW YOU'RE TELLING ME THE TWELFTH ONE CAME BEFORE THEY DIED? THAT DOESN'T MAKE ANY--
SHUT UP. YOU'RE NOT LISTENING. THIS IS A MYTH I'M TELLING YOU.
MYTHS AREN'T SOME COLLECTION OF DATES AND BIOGRAPHIES YOU BICKER OVER LIKE A CLERK WITH HIS LEDGER.
MYTHS ARE STORIES THAT ONLY HAVE THE MEANING YOU GIVE TO THEM. SO LISTEN:

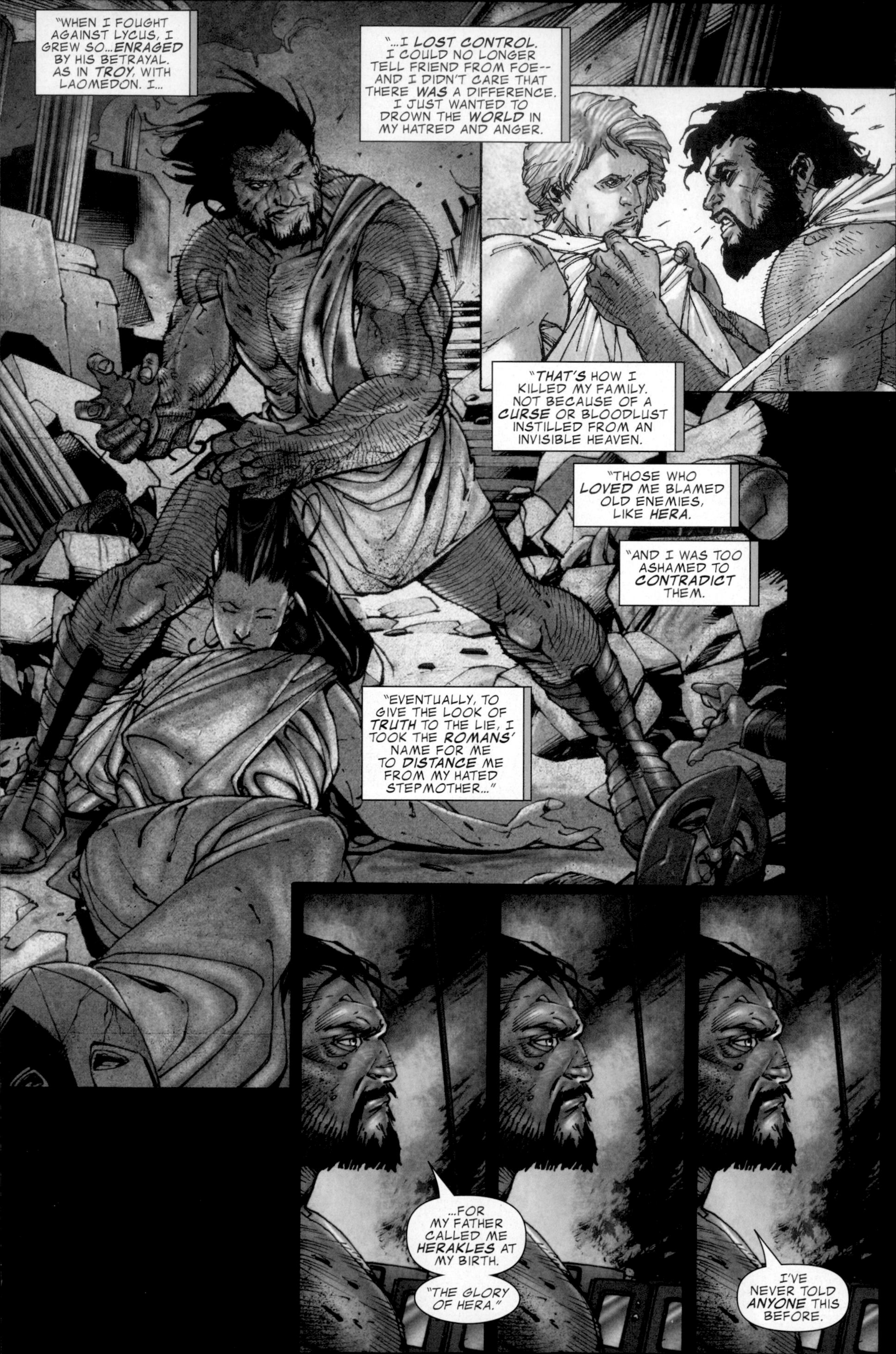
"WHEN I FOUGHT AGAINST LYCUS, I GREW SO...ENRAGED BY HIS BETRAYAL. AS IN TROY, WITH LAOMEDON. I...
"...I LOST CONTROL. I COULD NO LONGER TELL FRIEND FROM FOE--AND I DIDN'T CARE THAT THERE WAS A DIFFERENCE. I JUST WANTED TO DROWN THE WORLD IN MY HATRED AND ANGER.
"THAT'S HOW I KILLED MY FAMILY. NOT BECAUSE OF A CURSE OR BLOODLUST INSTILLED FROM AN INVISIBLE HEAVEN.
"THOSE WHO LOVED ME BLAMED OLD ENEMIES, LIKE HERA.
"AND I WAS TOO ASHAMED TO CONTRADICT THEM.
"EVENTUALLY, TO GIVE THE LOOK OF TRUTH TO THE LIE, I TOOK THE ROMANS' NAME FOR ME TO DISTANCE ME FROM MY HATED STEPMOTHER..."
...FOR MY FATHER CALLED ME HERAKLES AT MY BIRTH.
"THE GLORY OF HERA."
I'VE NEVER TOLD ANYONE THIS BEFORE.

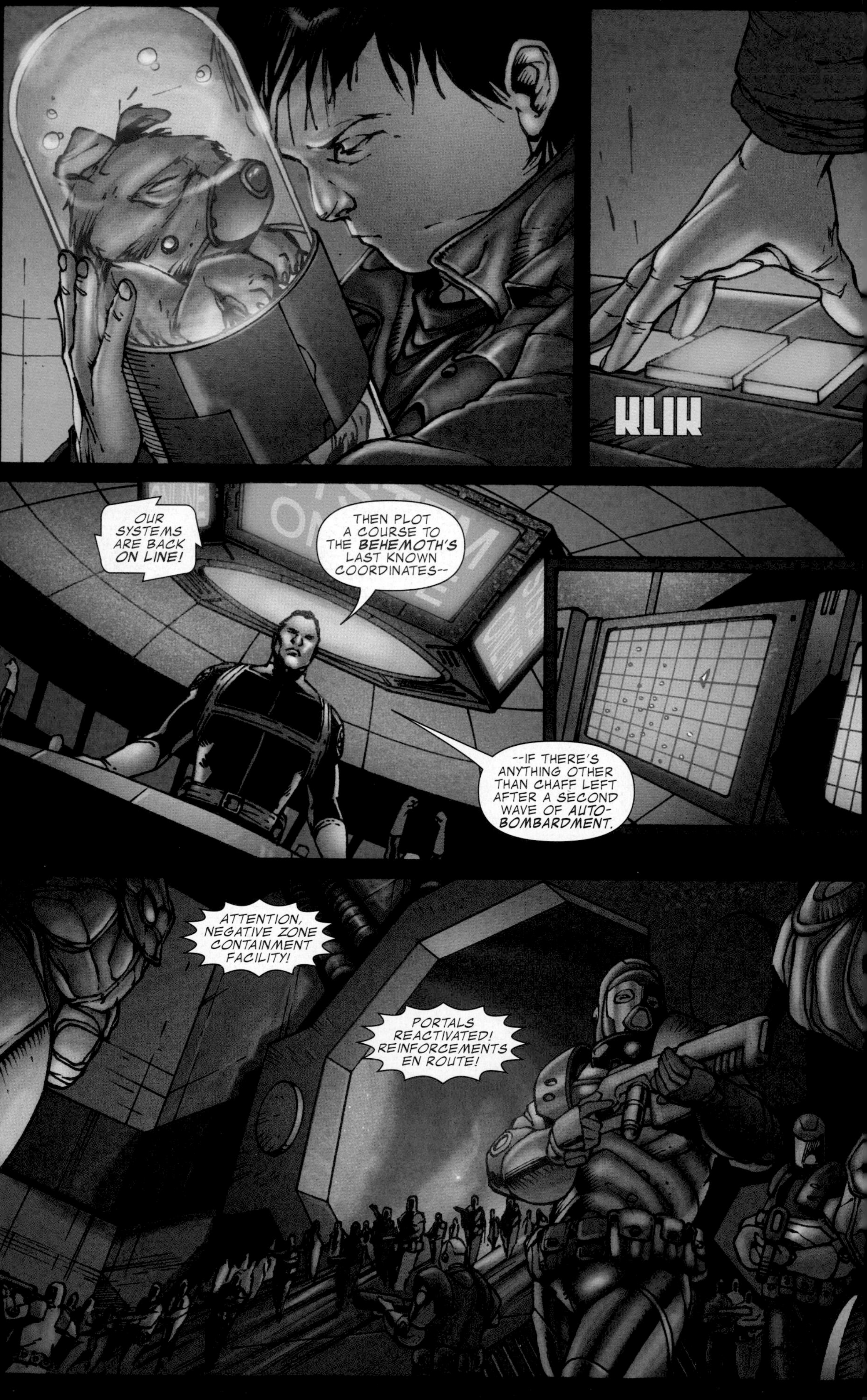
KLIK
OUR SYSTEMS ARE BACK ON LINE!
THEN PLOT A COURSE TO THE BEHEMOTH'S LAST KNOWN COORDINATES--
--IF THERE'S ANYTHING OTHER THAN CHAFF LEFT AFTER A SECOND WAVE OF AUTO-BOMBARDMENT.
ATTENTION, NEGATIVE ZONE CONTAINMENT FACILITY!
PORTALS REACTIVATED! REINFORCEMENTS EN ROUTE!

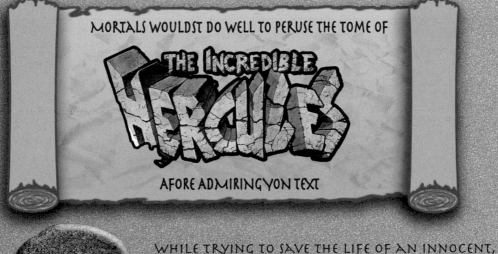

MORTALS WOULDST DO WELL TO PERUSE THE TOME OF

THE INCREDIBLE HERCULES

AFORE ADMIRING YON TEXT

WHILE TRYING TO SAVE THE LIFE OF AN INNOCENT, DOCTOR BRUCE BANNER WAS CAUGHT IN THE BLAST OF A GAMMA BOMB AND BECAME A RAMPAGING MONSTER WITH NEAR-LIMITLESS POWER:

THE INCREDIBLE HULK

FATHERED BY ZEUS, HERCULES IS A GOD AMONGST MEN, RIGHTING WRONGS AND DISPELLING EVILS. AND HE DRINKS BEER. CURRENTLY, HE IS ON THE RUN FROM THE MORTAL ENFORCEMENT AGENCY, S.H.I.E.L.D., ALONG WITH HIS SISTER, ATHENA, AND BOY GENIUS, AMADEUS CHO (WITH PUP IN TOW).

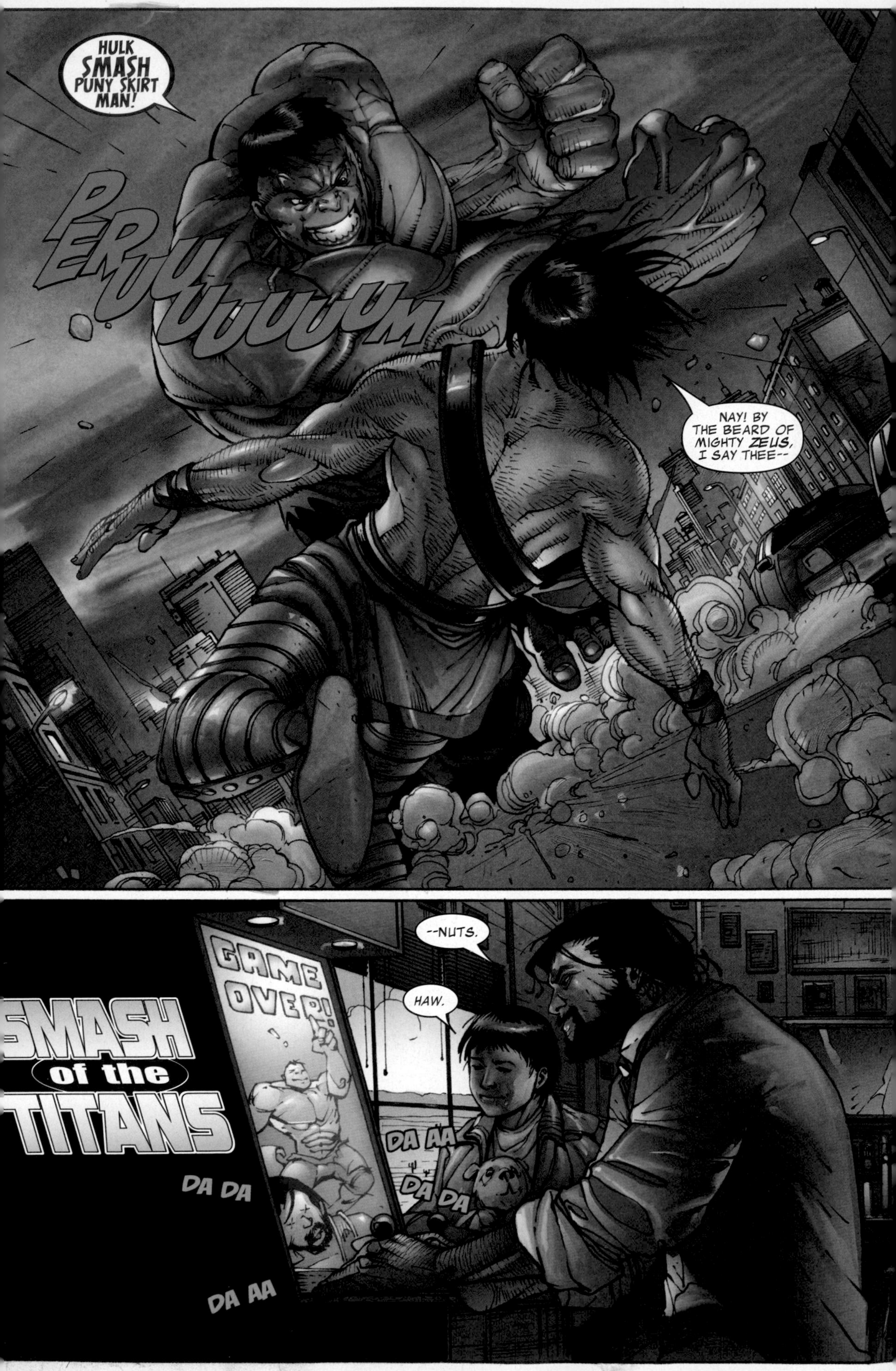
HULK SMASH PUNY SKIRT MAN!
PERUUUUUUM
NAY! BY THE BEARD OF MIGHTY ZEUS, I SAY THEE--
--NUTS.
GAME OVER!
HAW.
SMASH of the TITANS
DA DA
DA AA
DA AA
DA DA

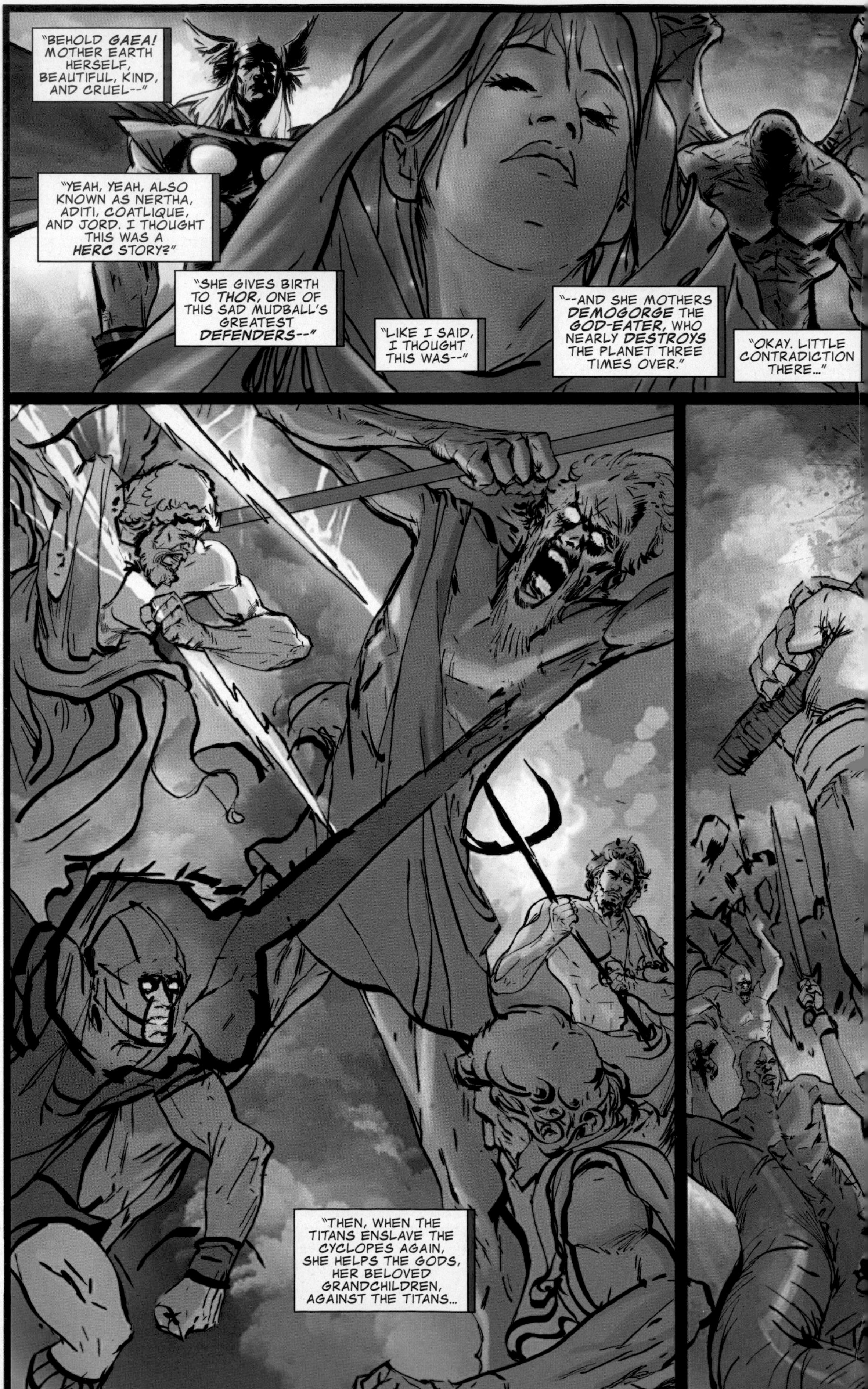
"BEHOLD GAEA! MOTHER EARTH HERSELF, BEAUTIFUL, KIND, AND CRUEL--"
"YEAH, YEAH, ALSO KNOWN AS NERTHA, ADITI, COATLIQUE, AND JORD. I THOUGHT THIS WAS A HERC STORY?"
"SHE GIVES BIRTH TO THOR, ONE OF THIS SAD MUDBALL'S GREATEST DEFENDERS--"
"LIKE I SAID, I THOUGHT THIS WAS--"
"--AND SHE MOTHERS DEMOGORGE THE GOD-EATER, WHO NEARLY DESTROYS THE PLANET THREE TIMES OVER."
"OKAY. LITTLE CONTRADICTION THERE..."
"THEN, WHEN THE TITANS ENSLAVE THE CYCLOPES AGAIN, SHE HELPS THE GODS, HER BELOVED GRANDCHILDREN, AGAINST THE TITANS...

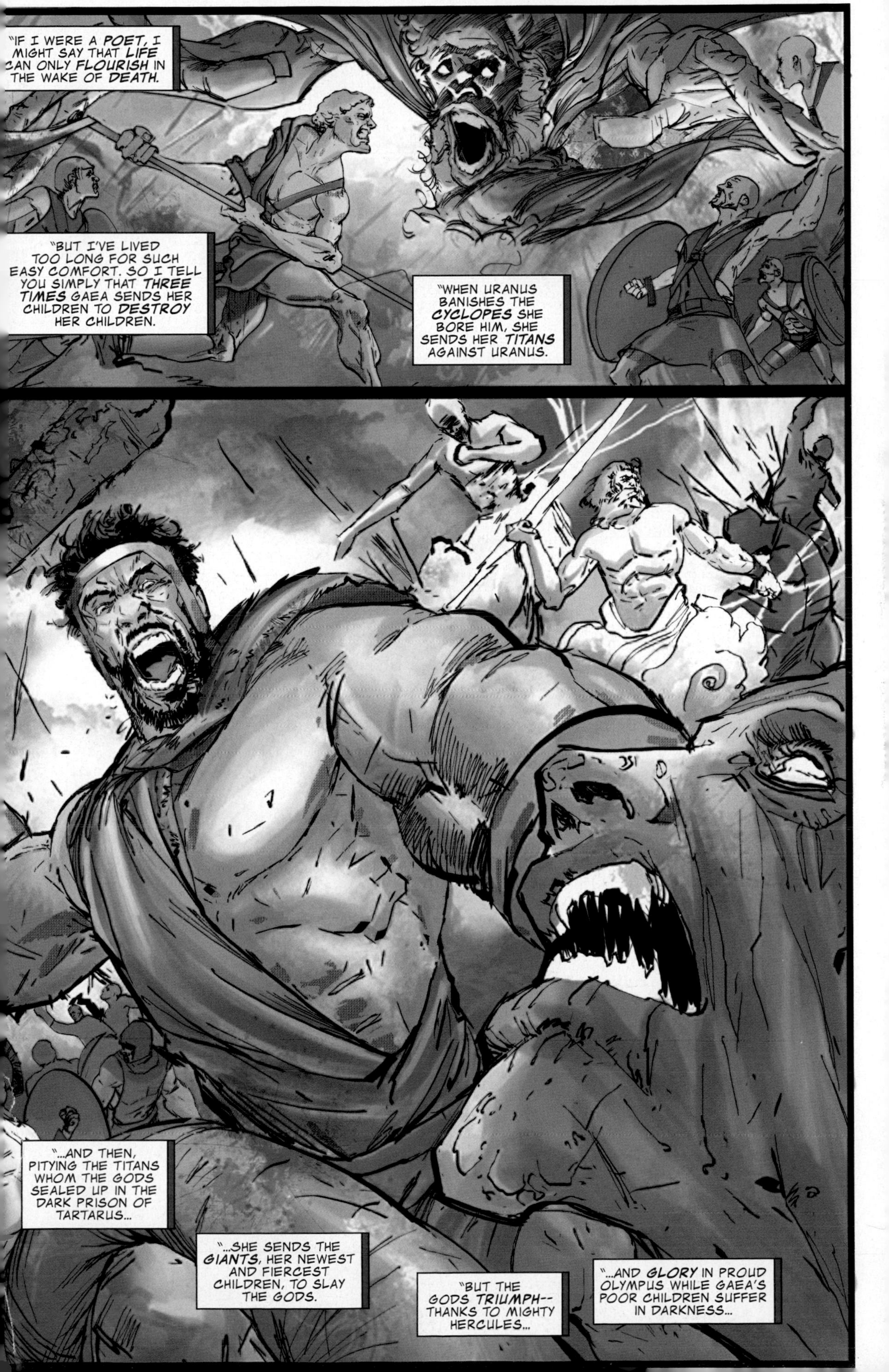
"IF I WERE A POET, I MIGHT SAY THAT LIFE CAN ONLY FLOURISH IN THE WAKE OF DEATH.
"BUT I'VE LIVED TOO LONG FOR SUCH EASY COMFORT. SO I TELL YOU SIMPLY THAT THREE TIMES GAEA SENDS HER CHILDREN TO DESTROY HER CHILDREN.
"WHEN URANUS BANISHES THE CYCLOPES SHE BORE HIM, SHE SENDS HER TITANS AGAINST URANUS.
"...AND THEN, PITYING THE TITANS WHOM THE GODS SEALED UP IN THE DARK PRISON OF TARTARUS...
"...SHE SENDS THE GIANTS, HER NEWEST AND FIERCEST CHILDREN, TO SLAY THE GODS.
"BUT THE GODS TRIUMPH-- THANKS TO MIGHTY HERCULES...
"...AND GLORY IN PROUD OLYMPUS WHILE GAEA'S POOR CHILDREN SUFFER IN DARKNESS...

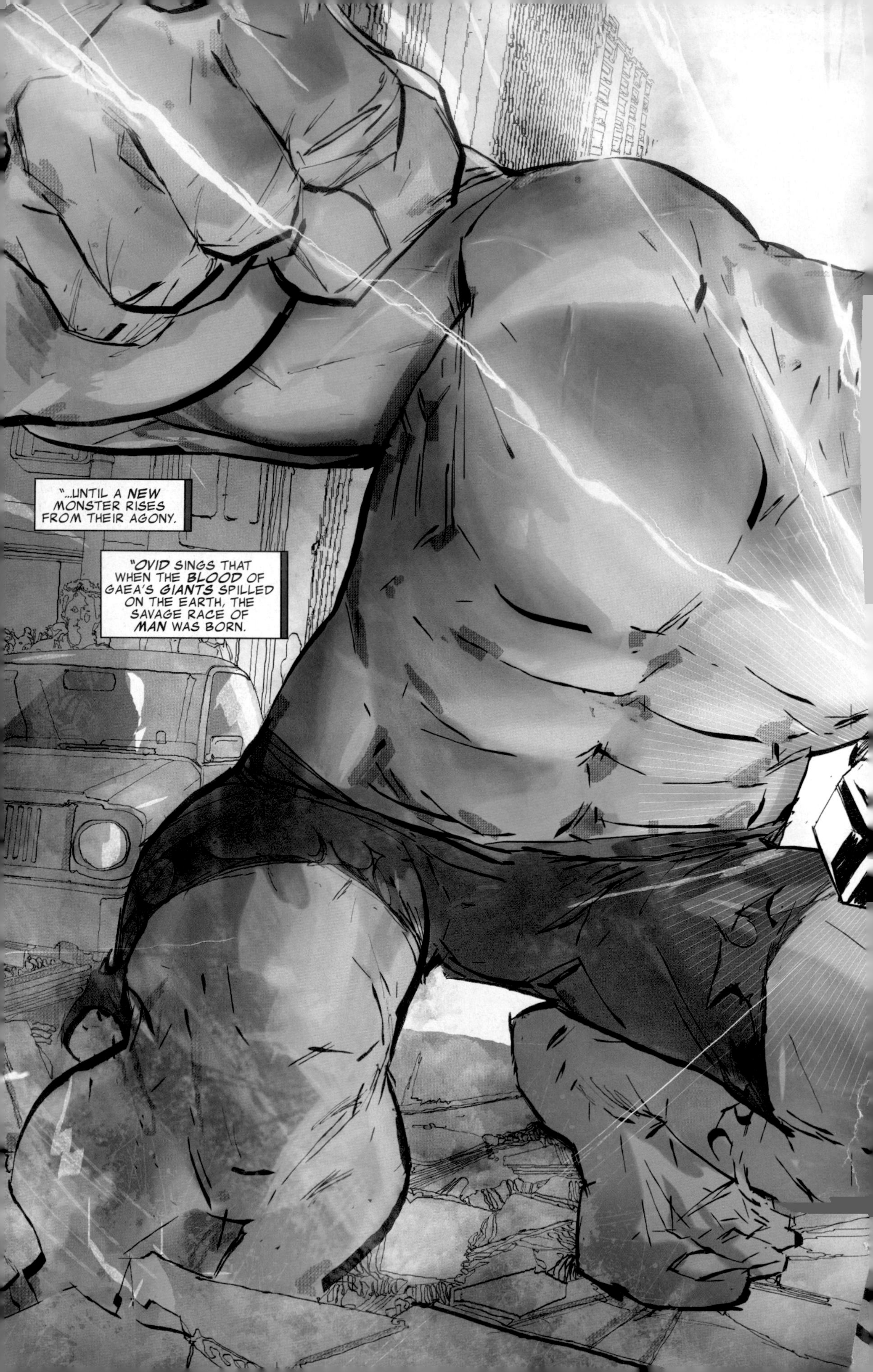
"...UNTIL A NEW MONSTER RISES FROM THEIR AGONY.
"OVID SINGS THAT WHEN THE BLOOD OF GAEA'S GIANTS SPILLED ON THE EARTH, THE SAVAGE RACE OF MAN WAS BORN.

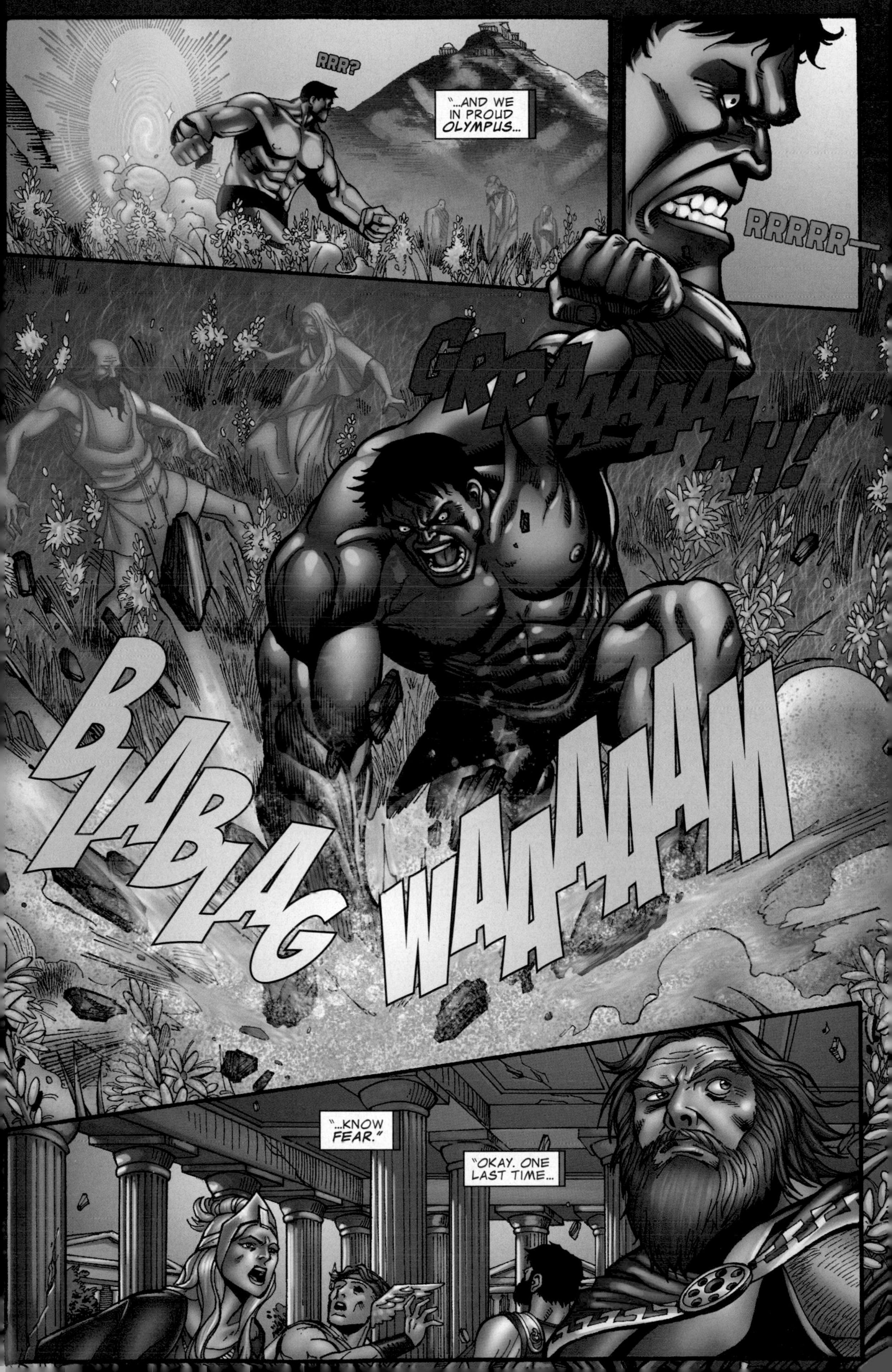

RRR?
"...AND WE IN PROUD OLYMPUS...
RRRRR—
GRRAAAAAAAH!!
BABLAG
WAAAAAM
"...KNOW FEAR."
"OKAY. ONE LAST TIME...

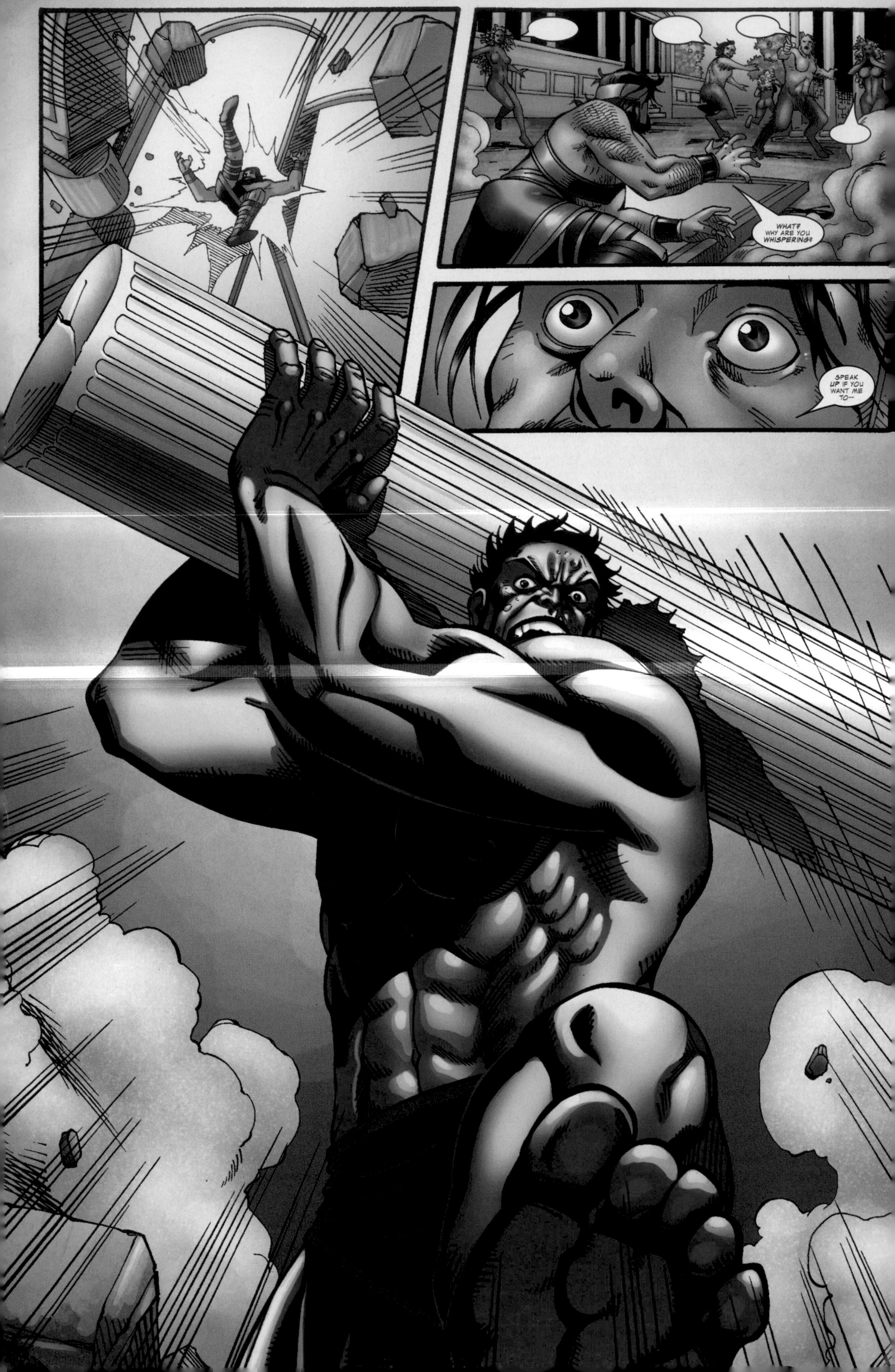
WHAT? WHY ARE YOU WHISPERING?
SPEAK UP IF YOU WANT ME TO--

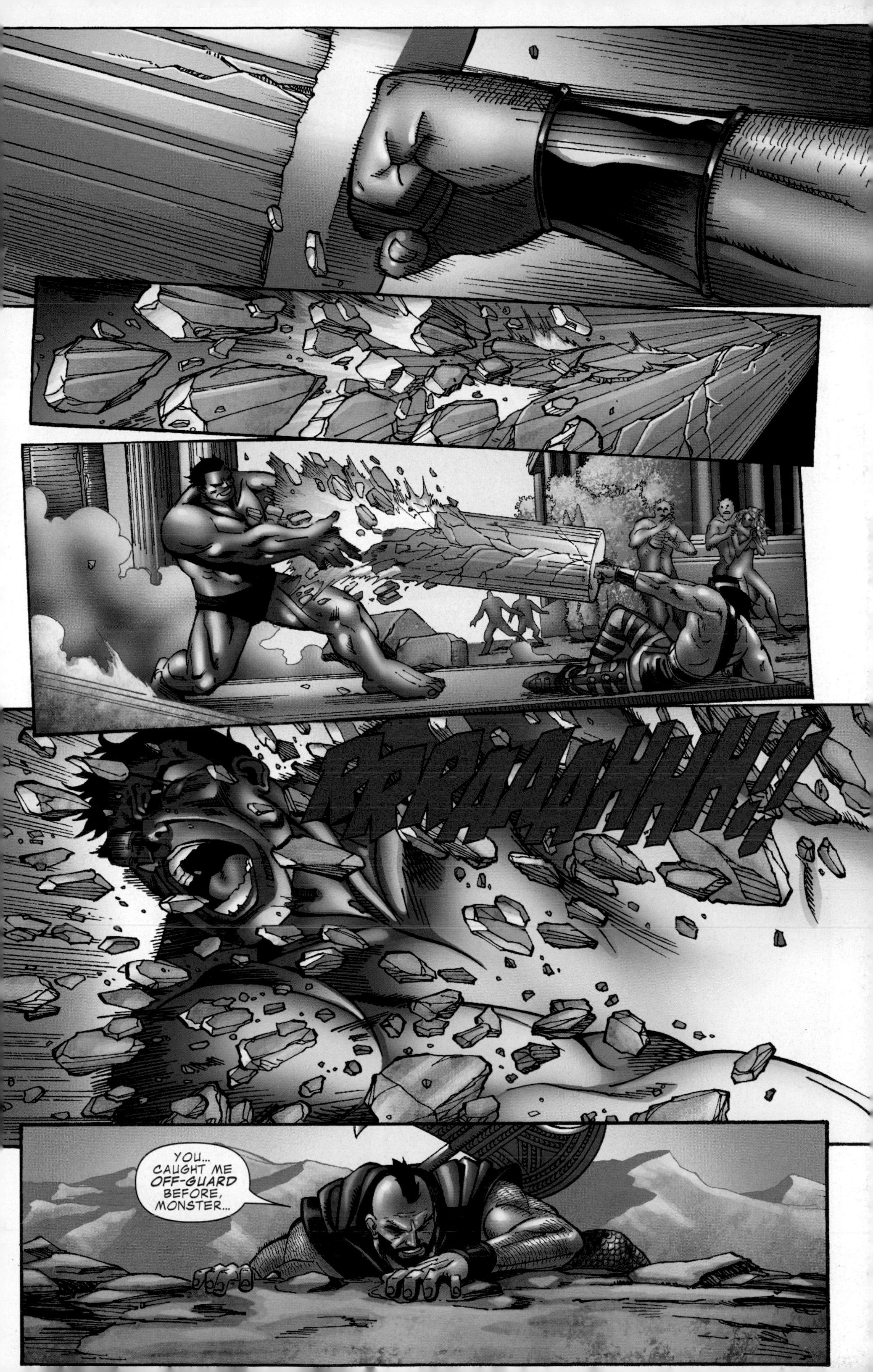
RRRAAAHHHH!!
YOU... CAUGHT ME OFF-GUARD BEFORE, MONSTER...

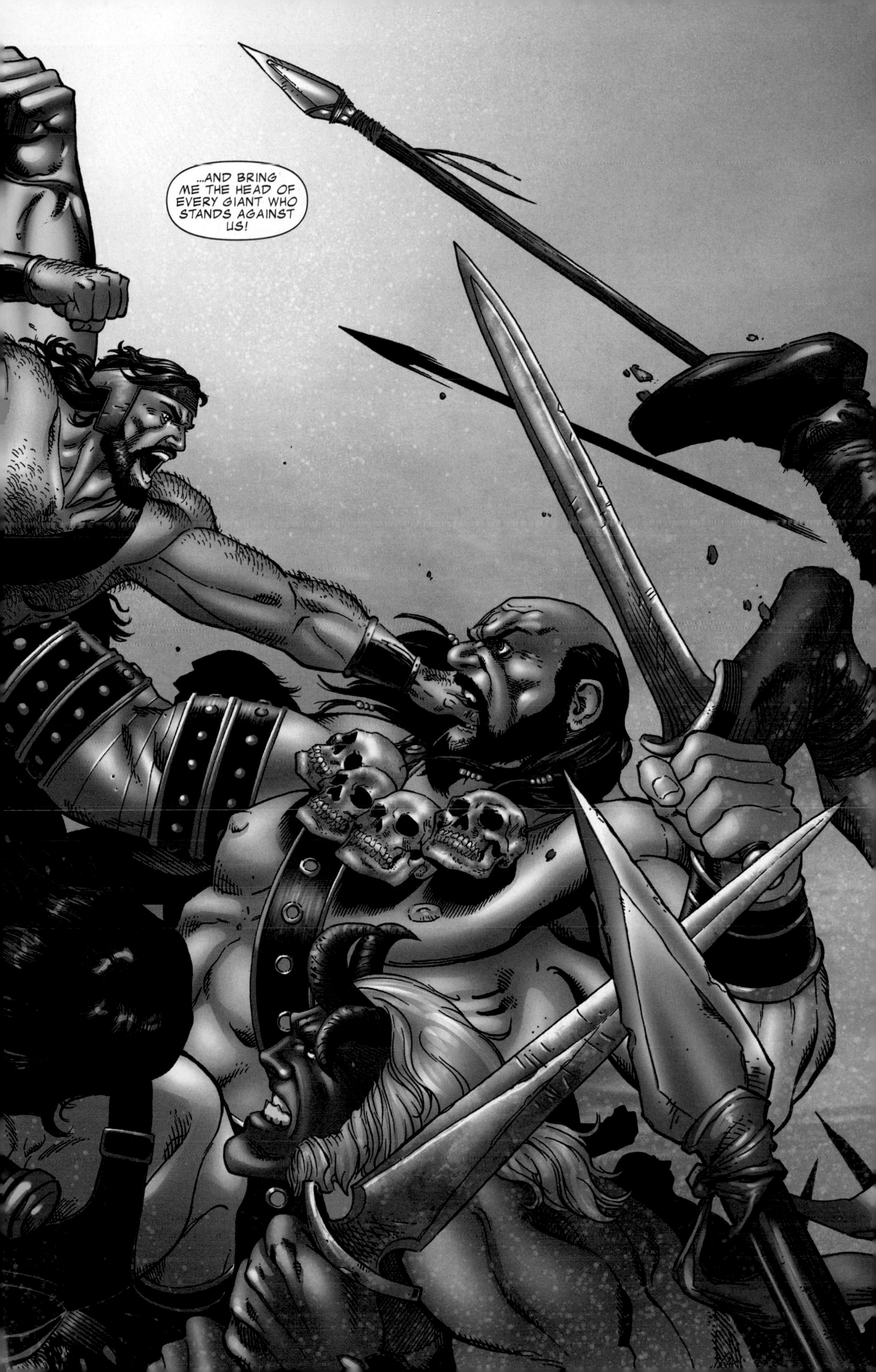
...AND BRING ME THE HEAD OF EVERY GIANT WHO STANDS AGAINST US!

END.